mercy like morning

JANE JOHNSON

HARVEST HOUSE PUBLISHERS
EUGENE, OREGON

Published in association with the literary agency of D.C. Jacobson & Associates LLC, an Author Management Company. www.dcjacobson.com

Cover design by Emily Weigel Design

Back cover author photo by Jenna Strubhar

Hand lettering by Jane Johnson

Photography by Jane Johnson

MERCY LIKE MORNING

Copyright © 2018 Jane Johnson
Published by Harvest House Publishers
Eugene, Oregon 97408
www.harvesthousepublishers.com

ISBN 978-0-7369-7315-1 (pbk.)
ISBN 978-0-7369-7316-8 (eBook)

Printed in the United States of America

18 19 20 21 22 23 24 25 26 / VP-JC / 10 9 8 7 6 5 4 3 2 1

FOR SHAWNA

Contents

Introduction 7

1. Desert, Discipleship, and Well-Digging 13

2. White-Knuckle Faith 27

3. Prone to Wander 41

4. The Learning Gift 61

5. Deep-Vein Mining 77

6. Deep Sea Singing 93

7. The Resources 115

   Sample Study 1: A Day in the Life 131

   Sample Study 2: Verse by Verse 157

   Sample Study 3: Rest: A Word Study 175

Epilogue 199

Notes 213

Introduction

Through the LORD's mercies we are not consumed,

Because His compassions fail not. They are new every morning;

Great is Your faithfulness.

"The LORD is my portion," says my soul,

"Therefore I hope in Him!"

The LORD is good to those who wait for Him,

To the soul who seeks Him.

It is good that one should hope and wait quietly

For the salvation of the LORD.

LAMENTATIONS 3:22-26

I was reading in 1 Chronicles 17 one fall Friday morning, eavesdropping on an intimate conversation between David and God. Life had finally gotten good for David again. Gone were the days of running for his life and hiding in caves from a previous king of Israel, who was bound and determined to kill him simply because God had handpicked the young shepherd to be the new king. It wasn't until five long years later that David finally took over the role. And his fame spread far and wide. And the people worshipped God. And there was joy and thanksgiving and a 1-Chronicles-16 party.

Late that night, as the worship party wound down, David made his way home. He likely took off his shoes and settled into a chair, letting out a deep 1-Chronicles-17 sigh—the way we all do at the end of a long day. As he sat there, he looked around his stately cedar palace, thinking of the transitory tabernacle-tent not far away. The one where the ark of God, and the presence of God, rested. And David suddenly got a big dream for a big God. He shared it right then and there with his prophet friend who was keeping him company.

David wanted to build a house for God. One that outshone his own. Because after everything God had done for him—the favor and protection and clout and provision—it was the very least he could do for God.

But a surprising thing happened: *God said no*.

He had other plans. And that night, as David laid it out honest—a king before his King—God quietly placed a holy finger over his well-intentioned lips and whisper-revealed the beginning of David's next chapter.

In response, King David sat before the Lord, acknowledging that he, in fact, had heard God's instead-plan. He prayed that the whisper-revelation would be established. "For You, O my God, have revealed to Your servant that *You* will build *him* a house," David said in 1 Chronicles 17:25 (emphasis mine). But the Hebrew word he chose to describe that whispered revelation is much more vivid. The literal translation is, "You have uncovered the ear of Your servant."

"You have uncovered the ear of Your servant."

As David sat there, God reached over and tucked every piece of stray hair behind the king's ear to make sure that nothing of His emphasis, content, or context was missed. He uncovered David's ear the way people do when they are about to share a secret.

But "uncovering the ear" is not the only interesting translation of that Hebrew word. That same word also means "to unfold a book." Much like this book you've unfolded today—a book of the lessons and whispered revelations that God has shared with me after tucking back my own hair. A book about how a combination of Bible curiosity and white-knuckle faith led to a cultivated quiet time of studying Scripture.

If I met you on the street and we began discussing the bare-bones basics of who we are, I would tell you this: "I am a woman who is caught in a passionate love affair with the Word of God." One that began with digging. And led to that tucked-back hair and, eventually, prayer-journaling every insight because I couldn't possibly remember it all.

You're there, with this unfolded book, having taken the first steps in digging up brand-new revelations of God's Word. Ones that are revealed to you by God Himself. And I'm here, standing on top of Psalm 96, singing a new song and teaching you the lyrics so you can sing with me and we can declare His glory together.

But that word *declare* in the psalm isn't only referring to spoken declarations. It also describes writing letters. Or, more specifically, it declares the role of the king's scribe—the one who is also a personal friend of the king, whose job is solely to write his letters, word for divinely-narrated word.

This book will teach you how to be intentional in your quiet times. It will teach you how to dig deeper into God's Word so that He can tuck back *your* hair for whispered revelations of your own. Ones you can write down and declare confidently as a personal friend of the King.

It's what Habakkuk did as he climbed his watchtower in the dark of night in chapter two of his book. He set himself on the rampart and stood his watch and strained his eyes to see what God would say to him. And the first thing God said after he climbed up that watchtower? "*Write.* Write it all down. Every single word I am about to tell you, *write it down.* Write it plain and clear and large and bold so that anyone running by can read it all in a cursory glance" (Habakkuk 2:1-2, my paraphrase).

When Habakkuk wrote plainly, the Hebrew language uses the word *ba'ar* to describe engraving letters onto a stone. It describes writing meticulously by digging out the sense and meaning of God's dictated words and then putting those dug-out words on public display. That same *ba'ar* word is used in Deuteronomy 1:5 when Moses explained the engraved-law-letters to the children of Israel—the law God Himself had carved into those two stone tablets. Moses took those engraved-words and explained them to God's people in more detail. Because *ba'ar* not only means *to engrave.* It also means *to explain, to declare, to dig out the sense,* and *to set it forth when dug out.* Which is how we find ourselves together here today, as I lay out all these Truth-treasures that I've dug up and dug out over the years.

Using the vast variety of Bible-digging tools available today, you can take any part of Scripture, roll it over in your mind, and discover something you haven't seen before— even if you've read it a hundred times. Throughout generations, God has given divine inspiration to Bible scholars who were hungry to learn more about His Word. And there are countless new insights yet to be discovered.

Because the depths of the riches and wisdom and knowledge of God are unsearchable, unfathomable, and untraceable (Romans 11:33, my paraphrase), you will never be able to dig deep enough. There will still be more treasures and wisdom and knowledge waiting to be found.

I could simply share with you the treasures I've discovered, the ones I've dug out from the depths of Him.

But I'd rather give you the treasure map.

These are the things I learned the hard way.

Or maybe I learned them the easy way. The natural way. After digging in deep when life got hard.

This book will teach you how to be a scribe. An engraver. A treasure hunter. It will teach you to dig out Truth from the Rock that is higher than you. It will help you recognize God's voice in your life as He tucks back your hair for those whispered revelations. And it will lead you into your own passionate love affair with God and His Word.

For from Him, all these insights and inspirations and ideas originate.

And through Him, they exist.

And to Him, they are directed.

To Him be the glory and honor forever.

CHAPTER *one*

Desert, Discipleship,
& Well-Digging

"Dig your well for yourself," she said, "and also for the people who follow along after you. And do it now, while you are single and can dig a little bit deeper and linger a little bit longer." She had a point. I really had nothing else to do but pass the hours drinking coffee, studying for exams, working my part-time job, and dreaming of how the rest of my life would shape up.

Shawna had been digging her own well for years with regular quiet times, letting God fill it with the water of His Word. And on those afternoons, I sipped her handmade iced coffee and drank from her dug-out-well wisdom.

Of all the things she taught me, that was what stuck. To dig down—and dig deep. Every day, coming to God's presence whether or not I wanted to, whether or not I had the time or the inclination. In the good days and the ones full of tears. *Dig in and dig down and dig deep into His Word.* So that when life got busy, and there was marriage and a mortgage and little ones at my morning-feet, I could draw from my dug-out-daily well.

And when I walked through the desert, I could drink from it.

I MET JOSH on a Tuesday evening in the spring of 2001. We stood outside Arnold Dining Hall—an ordinary, single-story cinder block building that sat on the southeast corner of the Oregon State campus. A dear friend introduced us in the ordinary "Josh, this is Jane" kind of way that forever changes the trajectory of your life.

I was 21, with trendy brown lips and hair sheared short. I smiled, and the butterflies quickly found their wings in my stomach.

"It was love at first sight for her," Josh loves to tell people. And it was. But it wasn't quite time for us yet, and those early butterflies quickly settled into an easy friendship marked with familiar bickering banter and near-constant togetherness.

Almost two years had gone by when I snuck through the side door of a darkened church, late for a midweek service. The sanctuary was full, and many people were standing along the back and side walls. As I made my way through the dark, looking for a seat, I caught a glimpse of a man out of the corner of my eye. The kind of corner-eye glimpse that makes you do a double take.

The man wore a ribbed, burnt-orange, mock-turtleneck sweater and jeans. He stood with one foot propped up on the wall behind him and a messenger bag slung over his shoulder and across his body.

Who is that? I thought, my curiosity piqued. I cringed when I recognized his face in the darkness. I had just done a double take on Josh Johnson.

That was strange, I thought.

Shaking it off, I focused on the service. But try as I might, I couldn't shake off the story that God had already written for us. And my easy friendship with him slowly began finding its way back to those early butterflies.

It didn't take long for the butterflies to be replaced with anxiety. A high school relationship had left me wary—especially of someone with as much charm and charisma as Josh Johnson. I played the classic cat-and-mouse game that every man hates. I couldn't decide between *Let's hang out every minute* and *Wait, I need space.* I gave the poor man constant mixed messages as I tried to figure out whether or not I was in love with my best friend.

We were a week into the "I need space" end of the pendulum swing when I found myself in the delivery room of a hospital, photographing the birth of a girlfriend's baby. My friend had been in labor for hours when that sweet babe stopped tolerating it and the room filled with a flurry of chaos and preparation for the last-minute cesarean section. A nurse handed me a pair of scrubs and led me into the operating room.

I kept one eye on the baby and one eye on my friend. The blue shield blocked her view, and she looked up at her husband as he stroked her hair and watched their daughter being born. In those brief miracle-moments, I imagined myself in her place someday.

And I couldn't imagine anyone standing beside me but Josh.

I called him later that night from the hospital parking garage, stuttering and stammering my way through the awkward and terrifyingly vulnerable words: "I think I want to try this. I think I want to try *us*."

Six months later, he slipped a ring on my finger.

And six months after that, I slipped into his last name.

FOUR MONTHS AFTER we got married, Josh and I moved to the same mountain town where Shawna and I had first connected. Slowly, over time, my life stage started to look a little bit more like hers. And slowly, over time, our discipleship relationship started to look more like a very close friendship.

By then, quiet times were routine for me. I was raised going to church. My parents' intentional prioritization of Sunday morning worship took root early, and there was never a time in my life that I turned my back on God. My relationship with Him was always the quiet, murmuring background noise—even when things got a little muddy.

Try as I might, I couldn't shake off the story God had already written for us.

Shawna's discipleship, combined with weekly student gatherings in that dining-hall-turned-tabernacle and regular studies with a handful of girlfriends, helped to facilitate a habit of mornings with my nose in my Bible, digging into Scripture while digging my well. Morning by morning, I took my perch in the same chair at our kitchen table. Reading passages, journaling observations, praying applications, rinse and repeat.

But after a while, I wanted to know more. I *craved* knowing more. And the simple read-journal-pray routine just didn't cut it.

So I started digging deeper. I looked up word definitions, I cross-referenced, I devoured commentaries, and I scribbled color-coded notes in the margins of my Bible just to keep the flood of information straight.

And still, I wanted more. So I kept going—digging through the layers, getting to the most vital parts of God. Just as He started digging into the most vital parts of me.

IT WAS LATE on a Sunday night when Josh and I lay in bed, whispering in the dark. I had broached the topic of children with him a week or two earlier, and he had needed time to wrap his head around it. I've learned over the years that his brain tends to work that way—chewing and thinking on things for a time before jumping to any immediate solution.

And then, in the late-night quiet, his words came tumbling.

"I've been thinking about us having a baby for the last few days," he whispered as he held me close. "And about you being pregnant. And I really like the idea of it."

I felt like he was telling me he loved me for the first time all over again. The next morning, I gushed my feelings out onto the pages of my prayer journal, filling lines with prayers for wisdom and direction and provision and all the things you think about as you begin planning your family.

I ended my morning with six simple words. Words laden with so much unknown weight that I couldn't even begin to fathom what they would come to mean.

Now comes the hard part: waiting.

THE NOISE OF the coffee shop drowned out the conversation. Three months had gone by with no sign of pregnancy, and I sat across the table from Shawna, who was getting ready to move out of state with her family.

She wrapped nervous hands around the mug and laid her heart out honest, sharing things she had been stuffing down deep and carefully avoiding in conversation, the way you sometimes have to do when you are a pastor's wife living a fishbowl life.

"I need to start preparing to be a single mother," she said. It was a bomb I didn't expect to hear. I thought she was being a little dramatic. I had never heard her say anything like that before.

Never anything even *close* to that.

"What?" I said, at a loss for words. "How…what…wait…explain?"

But she just knew. She told me that her husband had been talking in his sleep, sharing carefully guarded secrets. Revealing unspoken intentions and the heart-truth behind an upcoming move. God, in His mercy, was preparing her for the worst.

Their family of four left that small college town shortly after. And two months after she dropped the coffee-shop bomb, she returned again. With her babes in tow.

She was suddenly single.

A YEAR CAME and went without even a hint of pregnancy.

And then two years.

By year three, I had purchased a new camera and was chasing another dream—finally putting my photography degree to work. I was ready to quit my day job and become a full-time photographer. Prayer journal pages were filled with business-minded things and other daily-life distractions.

But in all the new beginnings, I felt like I was swimming in a sea of sorrow. And I felt guilty for feeling that way. I was grieving as if I had lost a child—which I hadn't. Wasn't I being overly dramatic? I didn't know how to grieve something that was never mine to begin with. So I didn't talk much about the fact that I still wasn't pregnant almost four years later.

I watched as girlfriend after girlfriend moved along into her next stage of life while I sat there, stuck in a stage I had entirely outgrown but was unable to move along from. Every morning found me in the same perch at our kitchen table, digging a little deeper in my Bible. My quiet times slowly began making their way toward topics of suffering and affliction and weariness and waiting.

> I wait for the LORD, my soul waits,
>   and in His word I do hope.
> Psalm 130:5

My whole being Psalm-130-waited and hoped in His Word. But every month also held part of my hope. And every single month, I was quietly disappointed. Thirty-five months in a row. Then forty-nine.

It wasn't until we were four years into our wait that we finally started doing the fertility tests. I was poked and prodded as doctors tested every theory. I read articles and got acupuncture and listened to stories and explored every old wives' tale. I took my temperature and tracked my ovulation and was injected with dye. There were ultrasounds and scans and exams to boot.

"Now," he said, "we wait for God to do His miracle."

The afternoon phone call came while I was visiting with a girlfriend. I answered the phone as I sat cross-legged on her living room floor, anxious fingers playing with the carpet loop threads on the floor beside me.

It was a quick conversation. The test results were delivered and I swallowed hard, smiled goodbye, and made my way home.

That evening, I sat cuddled up on the window seat of our stairs, processing the doctor's words, when the familiar garage-door rumbling announced Josh's arrival home. He went through his typical coming home routine, putting his keys and wallet on the corner counter by the door, and walked halfway up the stairs, meeting me at my perch.

"There is a low-percentage chance that we will ever get pregnant on our own." I recited the words, still numb with the news.

I didn't know the exact numbers. I hadn't thought to ask.

He paused for a few moments.

"Okay," he finally said, simply and succinctly.

"What do we do now?" I asked.

"Now," he said, "we wait for God to do His miracle."

SHAWNA'S NAME FLASHED on the screen as the phone vibrated the alert of her call. I answered it quietly, in the middle of a bookstore. I shared the doctor's vague message as I wandered my way around the tables of gift books, absentmindedly brushing my hand across cheerful and airy life sentiments that padded the crushing conversation of a broken heart.

Two hours later, she called back.

"It just isn't fair," she said. "And I just keep telling God how unfair it is that He isn't giving you a baby!"

"I know," I said in heavy agreement, at a loss for any eloquent words.

"It really isn't."

"SO WHAT ARE you going to do?"

It was the inevitable question that was always asked after sharing that kind of news. We had three options in front of us: artificial insemination, in vitro fertilization, or adoption. But we chose option number four: *do nothing*.

Our decision was hard to explain to people.

We just knew, deep down inside, that we weren't supposed to do anything but wait for His miracle. To simply trust that God would make our babe in His time. And that steadfast trust left me feeling surprisingly trapped. The more time went by, the more I felt like I couldn't talk about the heartache of the wait, or the sheer *weight* of the wait. I felt unable to share the hurt of the unanswered prayer because we hadn't taken the steps to fix the situation ourselves. Trusting God was the bed we had made, so we just had to lie in it.

But when did faith become only action? When was it just…faith?

FOUR YEARS TURNED into five and still, every day, I morning-crawled to the throne of grace. Still waiting for my turn to mother. Still waiting for my first while mothers all around me were going back for seconds, thirds, and even fourths.

Morning by morning, I dug up His mercies. Digging my well deeper by the day. And continually unearthing treasures and promises—the kind that made my soul breathe out heavy with relief.

I studied the passage in Isaiah that described Jesus as the Man of Sorrows who was well-acquainted with grief, and I compared it to the Gospel stories of the same Man who didn't allow those sorrows to steal His joy. He didn't allow them to be an excuse to back out of ministry, to avoid certain social gatherings, or to stop loving people. So I determined to be the same kind of person acquainted with grief—to keep going to church on baby dedication Sundays and showing up to the baby showers with a gift in hand and a smile on my face (even though I would spend the entire drive home getting control of the ugly cry).

I dissected Hannah's story in 1 Samuel, returning to it again and again. With each reading I dug a little deeper, looking for a new detail I had previously missed. Searching for a new nugget to fill the emptiness. A new comfort to ease the weight of our wait. I read it in different translations and studied the original languages and listened to sermons and prayed through commentaries. And I did the same with Rebekah's story, and Rachel's, and Sarah's. I read in meticulous detail the stories of barren women, counting the years—sometimes decades—between their longings and their miracles.

The Scripture doesn't show the waiting. In Rebekah's story, you see Isaac marrying her when he was 40 years old (Genesis 25:20). In verse 21, Isaac prayed for his wife because she was barren, and she conceived twins. But we don't learn until verse 26 that Isaac was actually 60 when those boys were born.

Just like his father, he waited 20 years to become a father. And just like her mother-in-law, Rebekah was barren for two decades.

What is it about Abraham, Isaac, and Jacob? I wondered one morning, scratching ink on paper during another morning-crawl to my Scripture-well. *Why are those three names always together?*

I went back to Genesis again, and it hit me: Abraham, Isaac, and Jacob were father, son, and grandson, respectively. Each of them married women who were unable to conceive for at least 20 years.

The women who waited the longest for their babes birthed men whose lives made the greatest impact.

And then God whispered hope: The women who waited the longest for their babes birthed men whose lives made the greatest impact. The longer they waited, the more far-reaching their story was. And the farther God's glory stretched.

My mind wandered to the words at the end of Psalm 33:

> Let Your mercy and lovingkindness, O LORD, be upon us,
> in proportion to our waiting and hoping for You (AMPC).

I turned the words over in my mind. *His kindness toward me is proportionate to the numbered days of my faithful waiting.*

And those words blew new life into my otherwise faltering hope.

CHAPTER *two*

White-Knuckle
Faith

Shawna was a newlywed of barely six months when we hopped a flight to Scottsdale for a girls' weekend. She hadn't even taken a honeymoon with her new husband yet, but I had somehow convinced Scott that she needed to leave the kids at home with him and head to the desert for a couple of days with me. With birthdays a week apart, going to a country music concert was our celebratory tradition, and that year I upped the ante by suggesting an entire weekend away to see Kenny Chesney and get a tan and play cards by the pool. Our Oregon skin was begging for warmth and color. So we got our spray tans and our manicures and loaded up the car, turning south toward the airport.

I drove. CeeLo Green provided the ambient noise. And Shawna told me about the ulcer medication her doctor had just put her on. She had been having nagging stomachaches for a couple of years that both she and her doctors attributed to the stress of suddenly being a single mom and sole provider for her family.

"It's got to be ulcers," she said. She hoped the new meds would finally take care of the issue. After five years of picking up the pieces, her life was finally getting good again.

We stayed up late that night, watching Prince William's wedding to Kate live from our side-by-side hotel beds. And I woke up early the next morning to Shawna quietly sneaking back into the room.

"I slept terribly last night," she said, handing me a pastry and the high-maintenance latte I favored. "Stomach cramps had me up before dawn."

"I wonder why those don't go away?" I said.

LATER THAT MORNING, I scratched notes in my prayer journal. I read a morning devotional on my phone as I drank that hand-delivered latte and simultaneously groaned out loud, rolled my eyes, and laid my head back against the headboard in that "Of course!" kind of I-get-it, Holy-Spirit moment.

"What I need is a shift in perspective."

"Can you envy the answer to someone else's prayers?" I scribbled the devotional-words with resonating conviction. "That 'poor me' mentality creeps into my heart when God answers someone else's prayers more quickly than mine. Or when He responds to them with a 'yes' but His answer seems to be a 'no' for me, or at least a 'not right now.'"

"What I need is a shift in perspective."[1]

Those words became my morning prayer. And shortly after, we shifted out of our room and straight down to the pool.

We played a lot of cards that weekend. And drank in the Scottsdale sunshine. And sang our way through the concert. And relaxed in the hot tub. But I look back on the photos from that trip and see a pain behind Shawna's smile that I didn't notice then.

Before the airplane wheels touched down again in Oregon, we had our plans formulated for the next year's birthday concert.

"Zac Brown Band?" I suggested. She agreed. And we squeezed each other tight in the airport before driving away, going home in different directions and pockets full of friendship and memories and only-funny-to-us inside jokes.

TWO WEEKS LATER, I was driving to Portland. I had just come out of the mountains and into cell service when a text alert on my phone dropped a Friday bombshell.

"The doctor doesn't like the look of the lump on my neck," Shawna wrote. "Please pray."

My brain went into overdrive, flipping through the card catalog of conversations we'd had in Scottsdale, trying to remember something, *anything*, about a lump on her neck.

Did she say something in the hot tub? Or maybe when I was half-asleep in bed? Or at the pool?

I am notoriously forgetful with conversation details—it's something my husband loves to tease me about. But this? I would have remembered something like this.

In classic Shawna style, she had kept the discovery of that neck-lump to herself because she didn't want to worry anyone.

I met a girlfriend for coffee shortly after and swallowed the latte down warm, doing my best to engage her in conversation while my mind was entirely swallowed up somewhere else.

"So what's new?" I ask, feigning fine. *It will be nothing.*

But that friend knew me. She recognized the feigning-fine signs. So I recounted Shawna's words with an *I'm sure it's nothing* brush-off.

I kept a manicure appointment later that day at the same time that Shawna kept a doctor appointment. I sat there in a spa chair with hands in soapy water, staring up silent at a muted TV, not knowing that her simple needle biopsy had turned into an unexpected same-day surgery.

An hour later, I picked up my phone to see three words waiting for me on the screen—words that were heavy with read-between-the-lines significance.

"Where you at?"

It was stage four colon cancer.

She was only 35.

THE DAYS THAT followed ran together. A mess of furiously scribbled notes from oncologist appointments, CAT scans, PET scans, and pharmacy trips. The sun was barely sinking down behind the coastal mountains on one of those blurred-together evenings when I stood in Shawna's driveway and talked to my mother-in-law on the phone.

"How do I pray for a miracle for her," I choked out in broken sobs, "when I have this five-year-long prayer for a miracle of my own that is *still* unanswered?"

THAT YEAR WAS full of infusions and scans and diet changes and hospital stays and new-normal adjustments. It was also a year of consistent cancer growth, despite aggressive efforts to stop it. And despite aggressive prayers against it.

Shawna had another CT scan on my birthday, and we hoped that maybe this one would finally show shrunken tumors instead of growing ones. But it didn't.

My legs buckled under the weight of the news, and I sat on our family room floor and cried. For an entire year, I had been clinging with white-knuckle faith to everything I knew about God. Clinging to the fact that He is sovereign. That He is good. And that He is a God of miracles.

I white-knuckled His goodness when none of this story seemed good—on Shawna's side or mine. I white-knuckled His sovereignty after getting gut-punched in my faith. And I white-knuckled the hope that maybe, someday, He would work it all out for good.

That afternoon on our family room floor, I pleaded with God, only able to repeat the same three words over and over again:

Change Your plan.

Change Your plan.

Change Your plan.

Desperate for something, anything, to hold onto, I reached for my phone and found the *Streams in the Desert* devotional for the day. It was a favorite of ours during those months that Shawna spent fighting. The ones where we dreamed of a family for me and a cancer-free life for her.

The very first sentence of my birthday-devotional was a quick and firm response to the prayer I had just prayed: "The plans of the LORD stand firm forever, the purposes of His heart through all generations" (Psalm 33:11 NIV).

It was a sucker punch of sovereignty, and God began to whisper-reveal the same thing He had to David: *I have a different plan for Shawna.*

It was a sucker punch of sovereignty.

And as He did, He also whispered His birthday-promise for me.

I couldn't believe I was seeing the words that I read next:

> *Sarah conceived and bore Abraham a son in his old age, at the set time of which God had spoken to him (Genesis 21:2).* We must be prepared to wait on God's timing...It is not for us to know His timing, and in fact we cannot know it—we must wait for it.
>
> If God had told Abraham while he was in Haran that he would have to wait thirty years before holding his promised child in his arms, his heart might have failed him. So God, as an act of His gracious love, hid from Abraham the number of weary years he would be required to wait. Only as the time was approaching, with but a few months left to wait, did God reveal His promise: "At the appointed time next year...Sarah will have a son" (Genesis 18:14). The "appointed time" came at last, and soon the joyous laughter that filled the patriarch's home caused the now elderly couple to forget their long and tiring wait.[2]

One week later, Shawna had yet another scan. The cancer was still spreading. This time, in her liver. And this time, it was her birthday.

I opened *Streams in the Desert* again. And God continued the conversation He had started with me a week earlier:

You will come to your grave in a full age, as stacks of grain are harvested in their season (Job 5:26).

When the sun finally drops below the horizon in the early evening, evidence of its work remains for some time. The skies continue to glow for a full hour after its departure.

In the same way, when a good or a great person's life comes to its final sunset, the skies of this world are illuminated until long after he is out of view. Such a person does not die from this world, for when he departs he leaves much of himself behind—and being dead, he still speaks.[3]

Stunned by the words I didn't want to read, I asked out loud to the silence, "Lord, how do I even pray with this?"

I had never even thought to pray about death. I had only ever thought to ask for the miracle.

The devotional that day sent me to Job 5:26, so I went looking in a commentary on the passage to see what the scholars had to say.

> It is a great mercy,
>
> - To live to a full age, and not to have the number of our months cut off in the midst. If the providence of God do not give us long life, yet, if the grace of God give us to be satisfied with the time allotted us, we may be said to come to a full age. That man lives long enough that has done his work and is fit for another world.
>
> - To be willing to die, to come cheerfully to the grave, and not to be forced thither, as he whose soul was required of him.
>
> - To die seasonably, as the corn is cut and housed when it is fully ripe; not till then, but then not suffered to stand a day longer, lest it shed. Our times are in God's hand; it is well they are so, for he will take care that those who are his shall die in the best time: however their death may seem to us untimely, it will be found not unseasonable.[4]

After piecing together a script of borrowed words, I began to pray the kind of birthday prayer for Shawna that I never imagined I would. Rather than asking again for the cancer to disappear, I began praying that God would prepare Shawna for heaven. I prayed that as her body failed her soul would shine brighter. That as the winter of her life approached, an eternal spring would still rise in her heart. And that the closer she came to the end of her journey, the more clearly she would hear the immortal symphonies of eternal worlds, inviting her to come.

Job 5:26, the verse for the day, promised, "You shall come to the grave at a full age, as a sheaf of grain ripens in its season." I looked at the verse one more time before closing my Bible and saw the next line: "Behold, this we have searched out; it is true" (v. 27).

This whole idea of not being harvested until it is time—Job's friends had investigated it. The Hebrew word for "searched out" is *chaqar*, which means "to search in the earth by digging." They had searched it out and dug it out and thoroughly investigated it. And their conclusion? *It's true. Hear it and know for yourself.*

While Shawna was digging in her heels and fighting for life, I was quietly searching in Scripture, digging around for the right verses to pray her into death.

FIVE MONTHS LATER, she was at home, in hospice care. And I was at home, staring blankly at my closet, trying to decide what to wear to her funeral.

I sat down in my chair at the kitchen table for one last quiet time before Josh and I cancelled life indefinitely and made the long drive back to her. I had been sitting in this chair for seventeen months, begging God for Shawna's miracle. I had been sitting in this chair for six years, begging Him for mine.

For whatever reason, He had decided it was best to withhold both.

Why are You being so deliberate in not healing? I cried

"Why are you being so deliberate in not healing?" I cried angry tears.

angry tears as my pen scratched hard on prayer-journal-paper. *And why are You being so deliberate in telling me that You are not doing it?*

Before I could even finish writing the words, His voice spoke strong and clear:

So you can pray.

I immediately flipped back in my prayer journal to find the words I used when first I began praying Shawna into heaven and then returned to that freshly tear-stained page. Writing prayers, flipping back to look, and writing some more—until I had finished re-praying that prayer of borrowed birthday words.

And then we packed up the car and left.

THE DAYS TURNED into weeks, filled with eating and drinking and telling jokes and playing cards and watching movies in bed and stealing away private moments to release the waterfall of tears before coming back to love on Shawna some more.

Thanksgiving came along. Josh and I skipped the holiday with our families so that we could celebrate it with hers. She lay there in her master-bedroom-hospital-bed with a clear view of the kitchen, watching while we cooked.

Just before sitting down to eat, we gathered in her room and held hands and gave thanks and prayed. And then Shawna's daughter piped up.

"We wrote a list of things that we are thankful for in school this week," she said. "Can I read mine?"

She scampered off to her room to get the paper and returned to read her handwritten list. It opened the door for the rest of us to share our lists. It was a thinly veiled opportunity to collectively say goodbye—because until then, she hadn't let us. But that evening, she sat quietly in her bed, receiving the words with grace.

Then we sat down at the table just feet from her bed. We toasted her, and she chuckled every once in a while, drifting in and out of sleep with the hum of conversation and laughter providing a soothing white noise. And we took photos. Lots of photos, crawling in bed with her and snuggling up close, knowing they would probably be the last photos with her that we would ever take.

That evening, as we were getting ready to leave, Shawna's pain went up dramatically. I squeezed her goodbye, choking back the tears.

"I'm okay," she said with that familiar read-between-the-lines significance that comes with a discipleship-turned-best-friend relationship. "Love you, Janeykins."

EARLY THE NEXT morning, I woke up to Josh sitting on the side of the bed, frantically putting his shoes on. Shawna's husband, Scott, had a suddenly-broken phone after a routine software update had been performed. And on it? All those priceless photos from the night before. All the photos from those last few weeks. All the text messages and voicemails and the kinds of things that are all you have left after someone is gone. It was all inaccessible. Josh flew out the door to help Scott retrieve it all.

He had been sitting there at the kitchen table for a couple of hours, trying to restore the memories, when Scott called Josh over, needing help rolling Shawna onto her side to help alleviate the pain.

Josh told me later that when he went into the room, she began speaking quietly. Unrecognizable words beneath her breath. A holy conversation reserved for another audience.

Around that same time, I had just gotten out of the shower and felt a sudden and overwhelming urge to pray. I sat on the edge of the bed wrapped in a towel, hair still dripping.

Get lower, God said.

So I did. With bent knees and my head buried deep in that small space between the bed and the closet, I soaked the carpet with a mess of tears and still-dripping-hair.

Tell her it's okay to let go, I begged. *Tell her it's okay because nobody else can. Only You...she'll only listen to You.*

As I choked out the almost-wordless prayer, I suddenly saw myself standing in a crowd of people. They were cheering, clapping. And they were all dressed in white. Everything was white. *There was so much white.*

And I saw Shawna running.

And, for a moment, I was running alongside her.

Just then, my phone vibrated. It was Josh, on his way with the kids to pick me up. I threw on some clothes and put my wet hair up in a messy bun, and I climbed into the back seat of the car when he pulled up.

The iPad was out, and the kids were watching some sitcom with canned laughter, entirely unaware that their lives had just been forever changed. Josh adjusted the rear-view mirror so he could see my face as I sat behind him. He reached around behind his seat and squeezed my leg tight. I smiled at him in the mirror.

"I'm going to drop you off and take the kids to a movie," he said. I said okay. Before I got out of the car, he squeezed my leg again and kissed me more intently than normal because he knew what I didn't know. What the kids still didn't know. I walked up the rain-soaked driveway and into the house where Shawna's dad was on the couch, staring out the window, heavy and quiet.

Her mom met me right there in the entry to tell me the news.

Shawna was gone.

IT WASN'T UNTIL later that I put it all together—fitting together the timeline of when she died and when I was on the floor. It turned out that the moment she passed was the exact same moment that I was pleading with God, lost in that vision and the very holy privilege of praying my best friend into heaven.

I GAVE MYSELF a month—to ugly cry and grieve with jagged edges and adjust to the new normal of not being able to talk to someone who was no longer there. Of putting the phone back down after picking it up to send a text message to someone who will not receive it. Of not looking around the room to catch the eye of someone laughing with me at a mutual inside joke that is now only funny to me.

How is this good? I silently cried out. *How is this Your plan? Withholding the one thing I want most and taking the one friend I love most—how in the world is this good? How did You let this happen?*

Winter settled in, dark and cold, and with it a heavy cloak of heart-squeezing, breath-choking sorrow.

I didn't open my Bible for weeks.

Friends sent unanswered texts with verses and devotional quotes and all the sugar-coated idioms people share when they don't know what else to say. It all sounded so trite. I shook my fists at heaven and prayed out of pure habit—stammered-out words from a thoroughly-crushed heart.

How could I navigate the sea of grief when my body was so heavy? I couldn't swim; I couldn't move; I couldn't kick to keep my head afloat. I was numb and just wanted to sink.

Thank You, God, for Hebrews 6:19, I prayer-wrote. *Thank You that You are the "sure and steadfast anchor of my soul" (Hebrews 6:19 ESV), and You won't let me slip away.* I knew that He absolutely was not going to let go of me. And I refused to let go of Him.

I also knew that in order to live, I had to heal. And after that month, I began the slow and painful process of pulling myself out by climbing up that anchor-chain that tethered me to Him.

It was time to draw from the well I had spent an entire decade digging.

CHAPTER *three*

Prone to Wander

When I was seven, I wore an eyepatch. It wasn't the kind of pirate-patch like you would wear for Halloween. It was the Band-Aid kind that was decorated with sparkles and stickers to pretty it up and disguise the fact that it was, indeed, an eyepatch. I was born with an inherent laziness in my right eye that made it sometimes wander, eventually requiring corrective surgery. So I wore the prettied-up-patch over my good eye to strengthen the weak muscles in the lazy one before the procedure.

And so it was that if you were looking for seven-year-old lazy-eyed Jane, you would likely find me on the playground, using my good eye to peek through a loosened corner peephole of a sweaty eye patch.

But there was always a box of replacements waiting in a drawer of my teacher's desk. So I'd go through the rest of the school day with my good eye blinded, pretending to see normally when everything was actually a blurry, jumbled, and frustrating mess.

It's ironic that I ended up in a camera career that is dependent upon having a good eye. If you're looking for me now, you will likely find me sitting in front of the computer editing photographs—the weak-eyed photographer who trained her one good eye to see well enough for two.

When things are lazy, they are prone to wander. That's why a regular, habitual quiet time is so important: It staves off a lazy faith and protects against a wandering heart.

Before we go any further in this journey of learning to study Scripture, let's pause to recognize and acknowledge the things that prevent a rich and habitual quiet time.

Sometimes, it's simple prone-to-wander laziness. But not always. I can't tell you the number of conversations I've had with people who truly hunger for a daily, dedicated quiet time and are quick to provide a laundry list of reasons why it just hasn't worked for them—reasons that end up creating bruised shins from never quite clearing the create-a-habit hurdle.

Clearing that hurdle comes down to what it always comes down to: *You have to really want it.* You have to want it badly enough to overcome the opposition that comes against you. And boy, will it come. It's no accident that David described the table God prepared for him in Psalm 23 as being in the presence of his enemies. And what bigger enemy do we have than Satan? The last thing that little devil wants is for us to sit in the presence of God. He doesn't want us focused and intentional—eagerly and expectantly waiting for God's presence to be made manifest.

There are 24 different Hebrew words and 15 Greek words for the single English word *wait* in the Bible. One of them specifically refers to staying at home and expecting a visitor. Moses used it in Exodus 24 as he prepared to go up to Mount Sinai with Joshua to receive the Ten Commandments.

"Wait here for us until we come back to you," Moses said (v. 14).

It's the same type of anticipation you need to have when you approach your quiet time: Stay put and expect God to join you right there in your perch. Whether it's an over-stuffed chair at home, your kitchen table, or a table tucked away in a coffee shop, expect Him to come to you.

When we get into a daily, habitual quiet time, we begin to learn and recognize God's voice and expect Him to whisper-reveal Himself. That's powerful. And it's the last thing Satan wants. You better believe he's right there at our table that God prepares for us every single day, doing everything he can to distract, confuse, and create disinterest in the Word of God.

We're about to dig into the top five obstacles to a habitual quiet time. Each obstacle will be paired with a handful of verses that are turned into Scripture-prayers. Because praying with our own words is powerful, but praying God's Word is unstoppable. Using

Scripture-prayers in your daily quiet time is taking God at His Word and believing Him for the fulfillment of it.

It's time to stretch your legs, leap over the obstacles, and dare yourself to deepen your understanding of the Bible. You'll be blown away at the things you dig up.

I promise.

OBSTACLE 1: *time*

Time. It's quite possibly the most common excuse I hear when I talk to people about their quiet times. It's not that they don't *want* to read, but there just isn't enough time in the day. The to-do list is demanding attention. The kids wake up early. If I don't get to the gym first thing, I won't go at all. The dishes need to be done. The laundry needs to be folded. Social media needs to be checked. (And scrolled. And scrolled. And scrolled some more.)

The time-sucking obstacles are endless—and often, they are valid. Sometimes clearing the time hurdle is as simple as prioritizing how your time is spent every day. But there is one particular game-changing concept that isn't often associated with time that begs for attention: tithing.

Also translated "giving the tenth part," tithing is often associated with financial discussions. But the concept of biblical tithing is actually rooted in the fruitful produce of the land. The most often-quoted section of Scripture about tithing contains a command that packs a powerful punch. "Bring all the food-tithes into the storehouse," God said in Malachi 3:10, "that there may be food in my house" (ESV, my paraphrase).

What if you tithed your time?

David put it plainly in Psalm 23 when he described a spread of food fit for a king that was prepared in the presence of his enemies. If we stitch the two verses together, a picture begins to emerge.

"Give me your food-tithe," God says, "so I can make you a feast." But He's not asking for just any food. He's asking for the best part. The first-picked part. The perfectly ripe part.

Now consider this: What if you tithed your time? There are 1440 minutes in a day. If we gave God 10 percent of every single day, we would be sitting at His table for 144 minutes. That's nearly two and a half hours! When we give God a tithe of our time, we're giving Him the opportunity to take it and turn it into a multiple-course feast.

"Bring all the tithes into the storehouse," God continues in Malachi 3, "that there may be food in My house." But the thing with that storehouse? It's also called a treasure house. Can you believe it? Here we are at the very beginning of the treasure hunt. Standing on the you-are-here mark of the quiet-time treasure map. *And it all starts with making the time.*

If you struggle with finding time for reading God's Word, dig out some time to read and pray these Scripture-prayers. Write them on your mirror with a dry-erase marker. Put them on an index card propped up in your car. Pray over them daily. And clear that obstacle.

> "Bring all the tithes into the storehouse, that there may be food in My house, and try Me now in this," says the LORD of hosts, "if I will not open for you the windows of heaven and pour out for you such blessing that there will not be room enough to receive it" (Malachi 3:10).

> *LORD, help me to tithe my time to You. Help me to give You the first part of my day—the best part of it—knowing that You will come and open the windows of heaven to pour out in abundance. I want to test You in this, LORD. I expect You to meet me here. Acquaint me with Your Word, and allow everything else in my day to fall into place.*

> He said to them, "Come aside by yourselves to a deserted place and rest a while." For there were many coming and going, and they did not even have time to eat (Mark 6:31).

LORD, on the days that I feel like I don't even have time to eat, remind me to come aside to You—private, face-to-face—to rest and breathe and settle in for a while. Use my time to make me more effective in the things that are vying so persuasively for my time.

You prepare a table before me in the presence of my enemies; You anoint my head with oil; my cup runs over (Psalm 23:5).

LORD, help me to remember that You prepare a table for me in the presence of my enemies. You spread a feast for me every single day. Help me to prioritize my time so I can accept the daily invitation to sit down with You. Help me to set aside time every single day for You.

Teach us to number our days, that we may gain a heart of wisdom (Psalm 90:12).

LORD, remind me that my time on this earth is finite. Help me to deliberately begin each day with You so I can gain a heart of wisdom that will last for all my days. I want my numbered days to be worthwhile. Help me to choose to make them worthwhile by seeking You first.

Take heed, watch and pray; for you do not know when the time is. It is like a man going to a far country, who left his house and gave authority to his servants, and to each his work, and commanded the doorkeeper to watch. Watch therefore, for you do not know when the master of the house is coming—in the evening, at midnight, at the crowing of the rooster, or in the morning—lest, coming suddenly, he find you sleeping (Mark 13:33-36).

LORD, I do not want to be found sleeping when You come. Help me to stop allowing time to be the reason I avoid sitting down with You. You make it so clear throughout Your Word that we do not know the time that You will come back. And on that day, I do not want to be caught having set You aside for lack of time. Help me to make time for You today, God.

OBSTACLE 2: *priorities*

There is a certain amount of crossover between time and priorities (and prioritizing your time). The kick-in-the-stomach truth is that when something is important, you will make time for it. Another way of saying "I don't have time for that" is "That thing isn't as important to me as these five *other* things." Every single day, you assign your time based on the priority of everything that has to be accomplished in your waking hours. But remember this:

You always have time for the things you put first.

All throughout the Bible, God repeated one clear sentiment: *Put Me first.*

- Exodus 20:3—Put Me before all other gods.
- Matthew 6:33—Seek Me first.
- Luke 10:38-42—Choose Me over busyness.
- Deuteronomy 6:5—Love Me with everything you have and all that you are.
- Colossians 1:16-17—I am before everything, and I hold all things together.

The list goes on—that's just the highlight reel. And the proper response after just a cursory glance at His put-Me-first exhortations should be, "Yes. Okay, God. You come first." But a daily quiet time often gets put at the bottom of the to-do list—and it gets knocked off altogether if even one more unexpected thing is added on.

Unfortunately, putting a quiet time at the bottom of your to-do list means God isn't a priority.

I know. Those words sting. But there are enough consequences to neglecting a quiet time and putting Bible-reading at the bottom of the daily priority list that they need to be heard.

Paul began 1 Corinthians 11 with these do-as-I-do words: "Imitate me, just as I imitate Christ" (v. 1 AMP). Or you could skip over the middleman altogether and go straight to the imitation source. In order to imitate Christ, you have to watch Him closely. Study Him. Look at Him.

In order to imitate Christ, you have to watch Him closely. Study Him. Look at Him.

As you're setting out to imitate Christ, take another look back at Malachi, who also had something to say about priorities. When he wrote his book, the Israelites had been talking amongst themselves. They decided that worshipping God wasn't really all that important anymore. And God, through Malachi, had a very strong opinion about it: "When you say, 'The altar of GOD is not important anymore; worship of GOD is no longer a priority,' that's defiling" (Malachi 1:7 MSG).

You are part of a royal 1-Peter-2:9-priesthood and you have the special access to God that previously only Old Testament priests were privileged with. That's a big deal. And yet, even with an all-access pass to the presence of God, a quiet time often gets neglected and eventually forgotten.

Pray with me that God will help you make those quiet times a priority.

> "Teacher, which is the greatest commandment in the law?" Jesus said to him, "'You shall love the LORD your God with all your heart, with all your soul, and with all your mind.' This is the first and great commandment. And the second is like it: 'You shall love your neighbor as yourself'" (Matthew 22:36-39).

LORD, help me to love You first and everyone else second. Show me that when I put the needs of my family, boss, coworkers, clients, or friends ahead of the need for time with You, my priorities are backward. Help me to prioritize You over them so that I can love them well.

Seek first the kingdom of God and His righteousness, and all these things shall be added to you (Matthew 6:33).

LORD, help me to seek You and Your righteousness first. Before my spouse. Before my family. Before my career. Before the morning news and a nagging to-do list. Help me to recognize that when I seek You first, all those other things that are high on the priority list will fall into place.

Now it happened as they went that He entered a certain village; and a certain woman named Martha welcomed Him into her house. And she had a sister called Mary, who also sat at Jesus' feet and heard His word. But Martha was distracted with much serving, and she approached Him and said, "Lord, do You not care that my sister has left me to serve alone? Therefore tell her to help me." And Jesus answered and said to her, "Martha, Martha, you are worried and troubled about many things. But one thing is needed, and Mary has chosen that good part, which will not be taken away from her" (Luke 10:38-42).

LORD, help me to prioritize You over the distractions around me. The chores that need to be done, the people that need to be taken care of, the phone calls that need to be made. Help me to not be too busy that I cut You out. I don't want to check in with You only when I'm frustrated and flustered. Help me to sit at Your feet when I start my day. God, You know the things that are distracting me from You. You are in control of all of them. Help me to set them aside for just a little while and choose You first.

Where your treasure is, there your heart will be also (Luke 12:34).

LORD, help me to make You my treasure. I want to lock my heart with Yours every single morning so it's there throughout the day and not somewhere else entirely. Help me to value You most and everything else second. Help me to go to sleep thinking of You and wake up thinking of You instead of wealth or renown. I recognize that You are not prioritized in my life if all of my attention is exhausted with other things. Be my treasure, LORD.

OBSTACLE 3: *wakefulness*

I have a confession to make: I'm not a morning person. For years, being self-employed afforded me the luxury of waking up every day at eight o'clock. It's tough for me to get up in the morning earlier than I have to, and I have an abnormal aversion to setting alarms.

I love my sleep. That's just the truth. So it's not often that I wake up (and stay up) before the sunrise. But when I do, there's something a little extra special about my quiet times. Maybe it's the special stillness that hangs in the air while the rest of the world sleeps. Or the freshly brewed coffee, swallowing down extra warm and chasing the sleep away. Or maybe it's simply the sweetness of the morning.

Jesus set the precedent in the Gospels for waking up while it was still dark to get away and get alone with God. That kind of sacrifice requires discipline, but it yields immeasurable rewards. In the early morning when your guard is down and your brain isn't quite fully engaged yet, He is able to whisper a little bit more clearly, talk a little bit more vividly.

What if you pushed through the waking-up-early pain and allowed God to speak through your sleepiness?

I had a dear friend speak into my life a handful of years ago by sharing a dream she'd had about me. "I was caught in those dazed moments between sleeping and waking," she said, before going into the dream details that ultimately led me to a power-packed promise from God.

What if you pushed through the waking-up-early pain and allowed God to speak through your sleepiness, the way my girlfriend did? Her obedience in giving God the first part of her morning to pray through that dream and sharing it with me provided a faith-stake I could use to mark out God's promise trail as we continued to wait for our miracle babe.

You could start by getting up five minutes earlier than your normal wakeup time. Then, after a couple of days, ten minutes earlier. Then fifteen. And so on, until you have carved out enough time to make your quiet time a morning priority. And, ultimately, a habit.

> He came to the disciples and found them sleeping, and said to Peter, "What! Could you not watch with Me one hour? Watch and pray, lest you enter into temptation. The spirit indeed is willing, but the flesh is weak" (Matthew 26:40-41).

LORD, my spirit is willing to meet with You in the morning, but my flesh is weak. It's so hard to get out of bed. Help me to discipline my flesh to get up and seek You. I pray that You would rouse me from sleep, God. Awaken me in the morning with Your Spirit to Your Spirit. Help me to make waking up early a habit so that You don't come and find me sleeping when You have prepared a table for me.

> In the morning, having risen a long while before daylight, [Jesus] went out and departed to a solitary place; and there He prayed (Mark 1:35).

LORD, on the days that seem to be the most full, help me to get up even earlier to pray. Help me to see the importance of solitude. I want to be found praying when everyone else is still sleeping. Help me to seek You in anticipation of the work that You will do in me and through me today.

Take heed, watch and pray; for you do not know when the time is. It is like a man going to a far country, who left his house and gave authority to his servants, and to each his work, and commanded the doorkeeper to watch. Watch, therefore, for you do not know when the master of the house is coming—in the evening, at midnight, at the crowing of the rooster, or in the morning—lest, coming suddenly, he find you sleeping (Mark 13:33-36).

LORD, *I do not want to be found sleeping when You come. Help me to not use sleepiness as an excuse to not sit down with You in the morning. I do not want to be caught choosing a little bit more sleep over You on the day You come back. Help me make a habit of waking up with You every single morning, God.*

I spoke to you, rising up early and speaking, but you did not hear, and I called you, but you did not answer (Jeremiah 7:13).[1]

LORD, *over and over throughout the book of Jeremiah, You talk about rising up early to speak. But nobody was there to listen. God, I want to hear what You have to say to me. Help me to rise up early to hear it. Help me to recognize the power of the early morning and the presence of Your Spirit there.*

OBSTACLE 4: *comprehension*

I can usually tell whether or not I will like a book within the first few pages of it. If I'm not immediately engaged in or enthralled by the story, I'll set the book aside and choose another one. And if the topic is over my head altogether? Forget it! If I can't understand it, how could I enjoy it?

The fourth obstacle that prevents a morning quiet time is another one that I hear often: "I read my Bible, but I just don't understand it all the time."

Maybe you're struggling to make sense of a particular chapter in the Bible (hello, prophecy!). Or maybe you're reading an easy-to-understand story, but there doesn't seem to be an application to our modern-day world (like that talking donkey). Maybe you feel like you've heard it all before. Or, just maybe, your quiet time feels like trying to sprint through quicksand and getting nowhere fast.

God is faithful to turn on the lightbulb of comprehension when you invest the time to learn His Word for yourself.

No matter what your situation is, there's one thing that will help you clear this obstacle: the willingness to learn. One of my very favorite things about studying Scripture is that its layers are endless. Once you begin to dig, it doesn't matter how often (or how deeply) you do it—there is still immeasurable depth left to explore. God is faithful to turn on the lightbulb of comprehension when you invest the time to learn His Word for yourself. When you've read everyone else's words about it and decide to start discovering it on your own, when you stop looking at a quiet time as homework and start seeing it as an opportunity to dig deeper into the depths of Him, He will reward your effort.

Charles Spurgeon preached it honest and true in an 1879 sermon on reading the Bible. He talked about the feel-good, pat-yourself-on-the-back sense of comfort someone gets when they read a chapter. But that reading doesn't do anyone any good if there isn't an *understanding* of what was read. They might as well be holding the book upside down or reading it in the original language—it's all Greek to them anyway.[2]

Don't just read your Bible—read with an understanding heart. You cannot allow confusion to prevent you from reading your Bible, and you cannot read your Bible without understanding, just to check the task off a list. The Author of the very words we are struggling to read is standing by, ready to unravel the confusion. We must just be teachable.

> Oh, how I love Your law!
>   It is my meditation all the day.
> You, through Your commandments, make me wiser than my enemies;
>   For they are ever with me.
> I have more understanding than all my teachers,
>   For Your testimonies are my meditation.
> I understand more than the ancients,
>   Because I keep Your precepts.
> I have restrained my feet from every evil way,
>   That I may keep Your word.
> I have not departed from Your judgments,
>   For You Yourself have taught me.
> How sweet are Your words to my taste,
>   Sweeter than honey to my mouth!
> Through Your precepts I get understanding;
>   Therefore I hate every false way (Psalm 119:97-104).

LORD, I love Your Word. Help me to understand it better. Help me to get to the heart of the truth. I pray that You Yourself will teach me Your testimonies first and foremost. God, I pray that You would give me understanding of Your Word. As I chew on it and think on it, may Your words break down for me in their simplest and purest form.

I said, "Age should speak, and multitude of years should teach wisdom." But there is a spirit in man, and the breath of the Almighty gives him understanding (Job 32:7-8).

LORD, help me to remember that age doesn't matter when it comes to understanding Your Word. Young and old alike can gain the wisdom to understand it. I ask for Your Spirit today, God. Breathe Your breath on me, the breath of the Almighty, and give me understanding of what I am reading this morning.

If you receive my words, and treasure my commands within you, so that you incline your ear to wisdom, and apply your heart to understanding; yes, if you cry out for discernment, and lift up your voice for understanding, if you seek her as silver, and search for her as for hidden treasures; then you will understand the fear of the LORD, and find the knowledge of God. For the LORD gives wisdom; from His mouth come knowledge and understanding (Proverbs 2:1-6).

LORD, I treasure Your Word, and I cry out for discernment today. I lift up my voice and ask that You would allow me to understand Your Word so that I can gain knowledge of You. God, I pray that You would make me knowledgeable in Your Word. Give wisdom today. Speak knowledge and understanding over me as I read.

If any of you lacks wisdom, let him ask of God, who gives to all liberally and without reproach, and it will be given to him. But let him ask in faith, with no doubting, for he who doubts is like a wave of the sea driven and tossed by the wind (James 1:5-6).

LORD, I recognize that I lack wisdom. I confess that I've avoided Your Word because I don't understand it. God, I ask for wisdom today, in faith, knowing that You give liberally and solely from Your desire to bless. Lord, would You give Your wisdom liberally to me today? Turn on the lightbulb of comprehension in my brain. Anchor my mind so that I can concentrate on You while I read. Help me to stay free of distractions. Thank You, Lord, that You give without reproach. I love You.

OBSTACLE 5: *sin*

Sin. It's the last and most dangerous obstacle against a rich quiet time because it is the one thing that physically separates you from God. Isaiah 59:2 says it sin-stark and honest: "Your iniquities have separated you from your God, and your sins have hidden His face from you." But the most interesting part of that sin-separation? The Hebrew word describes it as a veil. In fact, the same sin-separation word is used in Exodus 26:33 when God is giving Moses the detailed instructions for building the tabernacle.

"Hang a veil," He says. "It will be a sin-separating divider for you between the holy place and the Most Holy where I will meet with you and speak with you from above the mercy seat" (Exodus 26:33 and Exodus 26:22 combined in my paraphrase).

Even more interesting? That's the veil that was torn in two from top to bottom the moment that Jesus died on the cross in Matthew 27:51. His death literally tore up the sin-separation that stood in the spirit-space between us and God.

"Look," Isaiah continues in chapter 59. "When you pray and God doesn't answer, it's not that His power is lacking or His hearing is dull. It's the guilt of your sin that has shut you out from Him, severing the communication. And your sin itself has caused God to hide His face from you, so that He *will not hear*" (my paraphrase).

The same powerful point is plain and clear in Psalm 66:18. "If I regard iniquity in my heart," the psalmist says, "the LORD will not hear." Every single morning when you sit down to dig into a quiet time, God is ready, willing, and able to help in answer to prayer. But, as one commentary puts it, your sin causes you to "stand in your own light and put a bar in your own door."[3]

Even further, when you recognize sin in your life and then do nothing to remove it, it is impossible to regard, enjoy, or even perceive the majesty of God (Isaiah 26:10), because He has hidden His face, and you cannot see what has been hidden from you.

You can find Jesus in John 10 talking with some Pharisees—the kind of men who prided themselves on their fancied good works. As they talked about sheep and their true Shepherd, Jesus described the thief who masquerades as a shepherd. The one who comes to steal and to kill and to destroy by luring the sheep away from their real shepherd.

Satan's only goal is to lure you away from God, to steal you away from Him, to kill and destroy anything that connects you to Him. Not the least of which is your quiet time. And there's no better way to kill your conversation with God than to convince you that keeping your mouth shut out of shame for your sin is better than confessing it to the One who can actually do something about it.

The One who cleanses.

Who forgives.

Who offers abundant life.

Because, as one author puts it, "Satan dines on what we withhold from God."[4]

David tried his hand at sweeping his sin under the rug for an entire year. Not only had he slept with Bathsheba, but he'd had her husband killed so he wouldn't be reminded of the deed. But no matter how good you think you are at covering things up, "your sin will find you out" (Numbers 32:23). So God sent Nathan.

By the time Nathan showed up, David was exhausted from keeping his secret. In a confession that would eventually become Psalm 51, he let it all out. There is a beautiful simplicity in his words—one that replaces the hiding and withholding and secret-keeping and truth-avoiding with the fast and forever forgiveness of a merciful God.

So David said to Nathan, "I have sinned against the Lord" (2 Samuel 12:13).

And Nathan said to David, "The Lord also has put away your sin; you shall not die."

Oh, for swift and sufficient grace.

Your iniquities have separated you from your God; and your sins have hidden His face from you, so that He will not hear (Isaiah 59:2).

LORD, I recognize that my iniquities have separated me from You. Even if I did try to spend time with You, I know that my sins would hide Your face from me, and my words would ring hollow in Your presence. I confess my sin to You, God. Remove it from me, I pray. Cleanse me of my iniquities that I might see Your face and hear Your voice as I read Your Word. Forgive me of my sin, LORD. I don't want to be separated from You any longer.

Blessed is he whose transgression is forgiven,
    Whose sin is covered.
Blessed is the man to whom the LORD does not impute iniquity,
    And in whose spirit there is no deceit.
When I kept silent, my bones grew old
    Through my groaning all the day long.
For day and night Your hand was heavy upon me;
    My vitality was turned into the drought of summer.
I acknowledged my sin to You,
    And my iniquity I have not hidden.
I said, "I will confess my transgressions to the LORD."
    And You forgave the iniquity of my sin (Psalm 32:1-5).

LORD, my unconfessed sin has not only separated me from You, it has worn me down. It started out small. Inconsequential, even. But it grew over time, and hiding it from You didn't do me any good. Lord, I ask for Your forgiveness. I pray that You will forgive my sin that I have hidden for too long. Thank You, Lord, that when I confess my transgressions to You, I find forgiveness. Thank You, Lord, for Your mercy.

If I regard iniquity in my heart, the Lord will not hear (Psalm 66:18).

LORD, I know the sin that lies in my heart. I've seen it. I've ignored it. And I know that You will not hear me as long as it's there. So, Lord, I confess my sin to You. I will get out of my own way. God, will you restore our communication? I long to talk with You again. I crave a rich quiet time again. And I cannot have one with this sin hidden away in my heart.

When the woman saw that the tree was good for food, that it was pleasant to the eyes, and a tree desirable to make one wise, she took of its fruit and ate. She also gave to her husband with her, and he ate. Then the eyes of both of them were opened, and they knew that they were naked; and they sewed fig leaves together and made themselves coverings. And they heard the sound of the LORD God walking in the garden in the cool of the day, and Adam and his wife hid themselves from the presence of the LORD God among the trees of the garden (Genesis 3:6-8).

LORD, my sin not only hides Your face from me, but it makes me hide from You. I confess that I have been avoiding Your presence because of my sin. Rather than seeking You, I've hidden from You. I've covered my sin and tried to hide my shame but I know it's in vain. Thank You, God, that You still look for me. Thank You that You are ready, willing, and able to forgive me. Thank You that You still want to talk to me, after all that I've done. Forgive me, Lord. Thank You for Your grace. And thank You, Jesus, for dying on the cross for my sin.

CHAPTER *four*

The Learning Gift

I was tucked into a green velvet chair in the back of my favorite coffee shop when I discovered a cross-reference for the very first time.

Sitting cross-legged with a Bible open to 1 Kings 2 on the armrest and a worn notebook in my lap, I came to the Brook Kidron in verse 37. I noticed something I had never seen before: a small, italicized superscript letter that preceded the name of the brook.

What is that? I searched the page for the corresponding letter.

I found it in the center margin, nestled between the two columns of Bible-text. There were two other verses listed after it, and my curiosity was piqued. I pulled the ribbon marker over to the page to hold my place and went on the hunt for the first reference.

It was tucked away in 2 Kings, right in the middle of a story:

> He brought out the wooden image from the house of the LORD, to the Brook Kidron outside Jerusalem, burned it at the Brook Kidron and ground it to ashes, and threw its ashes on the graves of the common people" (2 Kings 23:6).

Confused as to what exactly was happening, I backed up and read the entire chapter for context. It turned out the King of Israel had sent a priest into the temple to count the money inside. While the priest was inside the temple, he found the Book of the Covenant, which had been buried down deep and long since forgotten.

The priest gave the book to a scribe, who read it to Josiah the king, who then called all the elders together to read it to them. And a good old-fashioned revival broke out.

It used to be that there was a regular out-loud reading of the book. But different kings over the years had become disinterested in it all, and the Book of the Covenant had been set aside and forgotten.

During the time that the regular reading had lapsed, the worship of other gods had slowly trickled into the Israelites' daily lives. But that was about to change. Josiah commanded right then and there that the priests were to bring anything and everything that was used to worship any other god but the Lord out of the temple. After it was all brought out, he fired the pagan priests who had encouraged the idolatrous worship.

After the priests were dismissed, Josiah took every single thing that was gutted from the temple and burned it. He broke down the pagan altars, pulverized them into dust, and dumped it into the Brook Kidron—sin and all.

Josiah kept going on that way until every single piece of pagan worship was destroyed—every pillar, every statue, every shrine. And then, King Josiah led the people in a spontaneous and unprecedented celebration of Passover.

Interesting, I thought, and then went hunting for the second verse:

> When Jesus had spoken these words, He went out with His disciples over the Brook Kidron, where there was a garden, which He and His disciples entered (John 18:1).

Once again, I needed some context, so I continued reading the rest of the chapter and found that this all took place the night before Jesus was crucified.

I remembered Paul's Romans-16-words. The ones that promise that the God of peace will crush Satan under your feet (v. 20, my paraphrase). And the lightbulb went on.

In 2 Kings, Josiah had taken the leftover idol worship dust—a physical representation of the sin of the people—and thrown it in the Brook Kidron. Then the people celebrated Passover. Hundreds of years later, in John 18, when the city of Jerusalem was bursting at the seams for Passover, Jesus literally walked *over* the Brook Kidron on His way to the cross. That brook of crushed sin was literally under the feet of the Man who knew no sin, and He was on His way to be sin for us, that we might become the 2 Corinthians 5:21 righteousness of God in Him.

But first, He celebrated Passover.

I sat still and stunned.

For the first time in my life, I had found an Old Testament story that connected to the New Testament, and I hadn't needed the prompting of someone else to find it.

> *That brook of crushed sin was literally under the feet of the Man who knew no sin.*

JOSH SLIPPED ME a gift the summer after the parking garage turning point that shifted our friendship into a good, old-fashioned love story.

I was neck deep in my newly-kindled love of Scripture-digging, and quickly outgrowing my Bible that was beginning to show signs of tattered wear. The standard page margins were much too small for the kinds of notes I was trying to write in them. And the cross-references that led me to that coffee shop, Brook Kidron moment weren't near enough in number for my liking.

I had just barely begun to look for a replacement—one that I could stretch out my study-legs in and grow into—when I looked at him in curious surprise, tearing at the paper wrapped around his gift. And waiting there inside the box was a brand new Bible. It was twice the size as my old one, with extra wide margins just begging for notes. I ran my hands smooth over the pages, breathing in their fresh, new-book scent.

The next morning, I started reading that new Bible in the beginning, at Genesis 1, with a brand new Bible-curiosity. I picked out a reading plan (see page 123) and made my way all the way through to the end, keeping an eye out for those cross-reference-supercripts, scratching ink on blank margins and making notes of my thoughts whenever I came across a treasure.

By the end of that year, there were verses underlined and promises bolded and journal pages dog-eared in "return to this" reminders. I closed the book of Revelation one morning and opened my Bible right back up to Genesis the next morning, determined to maintain the rhythm of morning reading and new morning mercies.

I had heard of a quiet-time method that would provide a little bit more structure to my morning study. So with a brand-new notebook and dedicated quiet-time pen added to my morning pile, I used a little bit of SOAP.

It's a well-known, tried-and-true four-step Bible-reading process that was originally developed by a Hawaiian pastor, and it's as simple as it sounds:

1. SCRIPTURE – Read your passage for the day from the reading plan, and write the reference at the top of the page.
2. OBSERVATION – Write a paragraph of simple and practical observations (who, what, when, where, and why).
3. APPLICATION – Write a paragraph about how those things can be applied to your life.
4. PRAYER – Turn it all into a prayer.

Wash, rinse, and repeat.

By the end of that second year, I had a notebook full of handwritten, soaped-up thoughts, but I was beginning to see that so much of it was just scratching the surface of what I *thought* a passage might be saying.

I started talking to Josh about going back to school again to get my master's degree from a Bible college. I didn't care which one; I just wanted to study the Bible more. As we began to explore options, Josh sent an email to the pastor of a radio show that he listened to often. He explained our scenario and asked if he had any advice as to the best school for the kind of thing I was looking for.

The pastor wrote back, giving a couple of options. But he also recommended a book, just in case we decided not to go the (very expensive) back-to-school route. *Search the Scriptures* was a three-year, one-volume Bible study course, and we found a used copy online for three dollars.[1]

"Try it out for a couple of months and see if it helps get you where you want to go," Josh said. It turned out to be just what I was looking for.

I liked the aim of the book—to help Christians young and old in their daily study of the Word of God. And I liked that every section had a couple of questions designed to encourage a personal searching of the Scriptures to discover God's message from each passage. And I especially liked that, though there were explanatory notes, they were kept to a minimum, the principle being that the truth we dig out for ourselves is more likely to be remembered.

I determined to get down deeper to the real heart of each portion of Scripture that I encountered.

I started the study just a few months after we started trying for our family. Though it was designed to be a three-year course, I wouldn't finish it for ten years.

I started *Search the Scriptures* where it began—with Luke 1:1. And I determined to get down deeper to the real heart of each portion of Scripture that I encountered—to the part I knew was buried down deep beneath my simple surface observations.

And over time, I discovered that there was more than one way to pick apart a section of Scripture, whether it be one verse (like a proverb) or an entire story (like a parable). In fact, there was much more than one. I've broken them all down into 30 individual steps that you can use to take your time on one passage in the Bible at a time, digging in and digging deep. You can apply one of these step-by-step prompts a day, circling the same passage with a different daily study direction. And then, before you know it, you will have spent an entire month on *one* section of Scripture!

30 WAYS TO STUDY ONE PIECE OF SCRIPTURE

READ IT ONCE, THEN READ IT AGAIN. Take your time to read the passage slowly, out loud, and more than once. If you're studying an individual verse, emphasize a new word during each reading. If you're reading a section of verses, emphasize a different verse. When you're done, every reading will have provided a slightly different perspective.

2. PARAPHRASE IN YOUR OWN WORDS. Before you go any further in your study process, it's helpful to simply paraphrase what you've read in your own words. This allows the passage to sink into your mind while you work to make it your own in the simplest of words.

3. READ A DIFFERENT TRANSLATION. Reading Scripture in different translations allows you to see how various versions have interpreted the original Greek and Hebrew languages in modern English. You can even compare various translations side by side for a broader understanding of the passage.

4. LOOK FOR AN EXAMPLE TO FOLLOW. As Christians, we are called to lead by example. It's a vital responsibility and one of the most important things to look for when studying a piece of Scripture—whether it's the example of men relentlessly ripping off a roof to lower a sick friend down to Jesus, or Mary's example of worship over work.

5. LOOK FOR A SIN TO CONFESS. As you study Scripture, there might be an illustrated sin that is present in your life. Stop and confess, making sure that you're experiencing genuine contrition over it. If you aren't, pray that God will soften your heart to get you to that place. And if there is sin illustrated that isn't part of your life, take prayerful steps to recognize it and avoid it in the future.

6. LOOK FOR A PROMISE TO TRUST. There are many, many promises in the Bible, so this one won't be hard—but make sure you are reading promises in their context! Freedom from sin and transformation into God's likeness

both come with knowing and trusting His promises. Look for a new one every morning that you can take with you through the day!

7. LOOK FOR A COMMAND TO OBEY. Did you know that there are more than 1,000 commands in the New Testament? They cover everything from your relationship with God to your relationship with other people, and, if obeyed, these commandments bring rich reward. Want to know more about the commandments of God and the rewards for obedience? Take a peek over at Psalm 19:7-11.

8. LOOK FOR A BLESSING TO ENJOY. Keep an eye out for blessings in the Bible, but make sure you don't confuse blessings with material things. Remember, Job had all of his riches disappear in a day. In fact, if you search for the word *blessing* in the English Standard Version, you'll see more than 100 results, none of which are tied to material possessions.

9. LOOK FOR A PRAYER TO PRAY. There is a lot of prayer in the Bible: Jesus prayed often, Paul includes many prayers in his New Testament letters, and Psalms is full of prayers you can apply to your own life. If you see a prayer to pray, don't just recite it. Dig deep for the heartfelt meaning, and pray with sincerity.

10. WRITE DOWN THE BIG-PICTURE SUMMARY. Recap why you think the section of Scripture you're studying is in the Bible. And, to keep it as simple as possible, try to sum it up in one sentence.

11. WRITE QUESTIONS AND RESEARCH ANSWERS. You will inevitably encounter questions as you study. As you research, be selective in your resources. Check the source as well as any statements of faith to ensure sound theology. A couple of good resources are www.biblehub.com and www.preceptaustin.org.

12. RECOGNIZE REPETITION. Rather than flying through your quiet-time reading, slow down and pay attention when a word or phrase is repeated (I even draw circles around them and draw connecting lines in my Bible).

Because when God says something once, it's important. But when He repeats Himself, it's really-pay-attention important!

13. LOOK FOR THE CONNECTING WORDS. Be on the lookout for words that create a relationship between ideas, stories, or parables. Words like *but*, *like*, *however*, *therefore*, and *because* are all important. Identify why the connecting word is there and the link it creates between passages to gain further insight.

14. CONSIDER THE GRAMMAR. In addition to those connecting words, the meanings and tenses of verbs are incredibly helpful in studying Scripture. Pay attention to where the action is, and note significant shifts in tenses (triggered by the connecting words) to pick apart those longer sentences.

15. DEFINE THE AUDIENCE. Knowing the original audience of a particular section of Scripture is just as important as knowing the content itself. It helps you to understand the overall setting and culture of the time period and provides the (usually unspoken) backdrop to a passage.

16. DO A CHARACTER STUDY. Pick out one character from the section of Scripture you're studying and dig a little deeper into his or her story. Find other places he or she is mentioned in the Bible and write a brief biographical summary. You can also look for one overarching lesson from the character's life to apply to your own.

17. RESEARCH THE AUTHOR. Has the writer of the book you're reading written other books? Are they referenced in other books? Knowing the author, their background story and experiences, and the timeline of when they wrote helps to shed light on the deeper meaning and intent behind their teaching.

18. CROSS-REFERENCE IN BOOKS BY THE SAME AUTHOR. Look for the same word, phrase, or idea in the immediate context of the passage first (recognizing repetition). Then, look at references by the same author in the

same book. Next, you can consider other books by the same author to further explain the same concept.

19. CROSS-REFERENCE IN THE REST OF THE BIBLE. One of my very favorite things when I study the Bible is to allow Scripture to interpret or explain Scripture. You can see what other authors have written about the same topic or if they refer back to another passage in the Bible. Cross-referencing also helps in recognizing the repetition of important themes.

20. OPEN UP A DICTIONARY. The meaning of words is incredibly important when studying Scripture. And while the original Greek and Hebrew are much more important to dig into, opening up an English dictionary is also helpful in providing additional insight.

21. PULL OUT A LEXICON. The lexicon of a language is its full vocabulary, including words and expressions. Using a Greek or Hebrew lexicon helps in understanding the origins and root meanings of words and phrases while also shedding light on the context and cultural meaning intended by the authors.

22. USE THE CONCORDANCE. You can quickly and easily find other places a particular word or phrase is used in the Bible by looking for it in the alphabetical list of a concordance, sometimes even located in the back of your Bible. This is especially helpful if you remember part of a verse but can't remember where it's located.

23. LOOK AT A MAP. Pulling out a map not only makes a biblical passage more real, but it also helps you to get an idea of the distance between destinations as well as the location of rivers, oceans, mountains, and lakes. Want even more detail? Look at a Bible atlas.

24. DO A WORD STUDY. Use an interlinear tool to see the actual Greek and Hebrew words used in a particular section of Scripture. Then, click on a word to see its original definition as well as every instance where it's used in the Bible! (Hint: You can find my favorite interlinear tool on www.blueletterbible.org.)

25. **RESEARCH THE GEOGRAPHY.** Going further than the physical landscape, a broader understanding of a land's overall geography helps certain passages come alive. Learning about an area's climate, as well as its seasonal and agricultural history, can provide rich insight into the narrative of a Scripture story.

26. **RESEARCH THE CUSTOMS AND TRADITIONS.** It's easy to insert our own culture into the context of a Bible passage where it doesn't belong. In this case, it's incredibly helpful to know the customs and traditions that were in place around the time that the passage you are reading was written (which can also help to unravel some of those New Testament parables).

27. **RESEARCH THE HISTORICAL CONTEXT.** Knowing the social and political climate of a certain period of time can also unlock a lot of insight into a passage. For example, understanding just how divisive relations were between the Samaritans and Jews creates a much richer understanding of the John 4 story of the woman at the well.

28. **READ A COMMENTARY.** Written by well-known theologians, commentaries provide additional insights that enable you to create an accurate application of any Bible passage through their verse-by-verse expositions and explanations. (Hint: My favorite resource is *Matthew Henry's Concise Commentary on the Whole Bible*.)

29. **LISTEN TO A SERMON.** Listening to a sermon is, by far, one of the easiest ways to study Scripture. But listening actively is a discipline. Put down your smartphone, shut off any distractions, and tune in to your favorite pastor's insights on the piece of Scripture you are studying.

30. **STITCH IT ALL TOGETHER.** Now that you've gathered a vast amount of information on one piece of Scripture, you can piece it all together into one incredibly detailed narrative and prayer.

I WAS READING Psalm 139 one morning. The words had been well worn and broken in and written raw in my prayer journals over the years. "My frame was not hidden from You, when I was made in secret," it reads, "and skillfully wrought in the lowest parts of the earth." But I wanted a fresh perspective. So I read the psalm anew in a different translation, and my eyes stopped short in curious surprise at the words. Where the NKJV read *skillfully*, the ASV rendered the word *curiously*.

I felt like Moses when he turned aside to look at the burning bush in Exodus 3, stopping to take a peek at the Hebrew word that was used there in Psalm 139. I wanted to peel back the layers of it and get to the heart of David's words. Asking the questions. Digging up the answers. Feeding the curiosity of what it means to be curiously wrought and intricately woven with bones and sinews and muscle and skin. Carefully and precisely, with painstaking accuracy and astonishing intricacy, in carefully concealed secrecy.

He made you fearfully, with astonishment and awe.

Four times in three verses, David talks about being hidden away during those early and growing months of a new babe's life. Each of those times he uses a *different* Hebrew word. Hedged in and covered over, in that secret place of the womb, God sat down at His workbench. He laid out His threads, pulling personality pieces and physiological parts together from His infinite collection of creative inventory.

And He began to weave.

He made you fearfully, with astonishment and awe. And He made you wonderfully—distinct and distinguished and altogether different, with woven skin-clothes of handpicked and carefully curated colors.

Marvelous are His works. That my soul knows very well.

As I continued to dig into the heart of David's Hebrew words, I found an interesting connection to the curiously-wrought phrase that caught my attention in the first place: the Hebrew word is *raqam*, and it's scattered all throughout the book of Exodus.

Long before David stood in fearful awe of God's intricate and meticulous weaving, God took His weaving-wisdom and instilled it in the minds of skillful and gifted artisans. The same artisans who helped to build the tabernacle in Exodus 31.

Full of God's weaving-wisdom, those artisans took blue, purple, and scarlet threads and fine-woven linen and sewed them together into curtains. They hung the curtains at the entrance to the tabernacle as the first thing Aaron (and his sons after him) would walk through when he entered to serve the Lord as priest. Those curtains also hung at the entrance to the Holy Place, and they veiled the entrance five layers thick to the Holy of Holies, where God spoke intimately with Aaron.

You were skillfully wrought to have an intricately woven curiosity.

And every single piece of clothing that the priest wore when he finally entered into that holiest place? It was all *raqam*-woven. Intricately. Skillfully. And curiously. And the thing about those holy-woven garments? They were passed on to Aaron's descendants after him, that they might also serve God in them the very same way. Intimately and purposefully. From generation to generation (Exodus 29:29).

That's the best part about the things that God tucks back your hair to whisper-reveal to you. The things that He uncovers through peeled-back layers and pushed-back curtains in those intimate, Holy-of-Holies conversations. They belong to you. And to your children—that they might also know the depths of God the very same way. From generation to generation (Deuteronomy 29:29).

You were skillfully wrought to have an intricately woven curiosity. To dig through the layers and get to the most vital parts of God, to explore the depths of Him who cannot be fully explored, to search out His ways which cannot be searched. Just to find His goodness.

"Blessed is the man You choose, and cause to approach You, that he may dwell in Your courts," David wrote in Psalm 65:4. "We shall be satisfied with the goodness of Your house." And the goodness he's talking about is actually *the goodness of intelligence* or *good understanding.*

Those words by themselves are a powerful promise. But a powerful promise-punch comes when you combine them with the story in Matthew 11 where Jesus offers a trade: His light burden for your heavy one.

"Blessed is the man God chooses and brings in to dwell and rest in His tabernacle," David says in my own paraphrase of Psalm 65. "They will be satiated with good intelligence and understanding."

"Come to Me," Jesus says in Matthew 11 (again my paraphrase), "everyone who labors and works hard and grows weary in the hustle. Everyone who is worked up and burdened down and altogether heavy. Come to Me and I will give you rest."

Then He offers that heavy burden trade-out. And once that weight is off, once you can roll your shoulders and stretch your back and revel in the lightness of it all, He takes it one step further.

"*Learn from Me,*" Jesus says (my emphasis), "I will teach you gently." The words of *The Message* twirl around in a gentle, light-on-your-feet kind of supernatural waltz: "Walk with me and work with me—watch how I do it. Learn the unforced rhythms of grace" (Matthew 11:28 MSG).

I chew on *the gift of grace* and *the goodness of intelligence,* and my mind instinctively moves to 1 Corinthians 12 and the list of spiritual gifts. There are a lot of things on that list—wisdom and prophecy and faith and miracles and all the rest. Things that are spread around and divvied up and Spirit-shared across Christians in one gift or another.

But there is one gift you won't find mixed in there: the gift of learning.

That, sweet friends, is open to everyone for the taking.

And so it begins—this learning how to dance and rest and dwell in the goodness of intelligence and understanding.

It's all a gift, really, and it's just as profound as it is simple.

And it's yours for the taking.

CHAPTER *five*

Deep-Vein Mining

It was the dead of winter when I found myself standing waist-deep in the crystal clear water of the Caribbean ocean just a few months before Shawna's diagnosis. I had just finished photographing an intimate portrait session with a bride and groom on the day after their wedding. We walked the beach, and they snuggled close, basking in the kind of glow that first-day newlyweds have about them.

We came upon an old wooden dock as the sun sank low. It was just far enough into the surf break that we had to time our approach carefully, watching the waves and waiting for a break to run out and jump up onto it so the first-day-wife wouldn't get her gown soaked.

We photographed out there on that dock tucked in the sea until the light was gone. At the very last minute, with the sky still pink, I handed my camera over to get a photograph of Josh and me sitting at the end of the dock. I wanted to remember that warm, tropical January evening in my red bikini with my most favorite man.

That photograph of us on the dock was eventually matted and framed in our bedroom, part of a gallery of our favorite marriage moments, forever tucked into picture frames for safekeeping.

THAT FIRST WINTER without Shawna felt extra cold. And extra long.

I craved someplace warm where I could step outside to catch my breath without the winter air catching it sharp like an icicle in my throat.

I needed a change of scenery. A place where the heavy winter clothes were packed away.

A place with a different quiet-time kitchen table than the one I had sat down at for seven years, pounding my white-knuckled fists on heaven's doors and begging for those sovereignly denied miracles.

I needed a place to heal.

When we began seriously talking about moving, Josh bought a map of the United States and spread it out large and flat over that pounded-on and prayed-over table. With a giant-sized permanent marker, we methodically blacked out the states that didn't fit our let's-find-someplace-warm criteria—starting with South Dakota and coloring right on into its northern neighbor (no offense to you Dakotans, but we hear those winters are brutal!).

By the time that next winter came along, we'd wrestled through the choices. Should we give into our wanderlust? Or should we be practical and responsible and move to a suburb with great schools for our someday-children?

We have the rest of our lives to be practical, we decided. It would be our last winter in Oregon. Come June, we were moving to Maui.

I STOOD IN the middle of our closet, taking inventory of what to take and what to toss and what to pack away in storage when I opened the dresser drawer of mismatched bathing suits and mysteriously orphaned socks. Buried in the back was that well-worn and now threadbare red bikini.

The fabric on the bottoms had separated and stretched, sagging. The top was faded. And it was time to part ways with my favorite bathing suit. No sooner was it thrown in the trash heap among empty toilet paper rolls and old fabric softener sheets than I started looking for a replacement.

I searched high and low in those last few months before we moved. In town. Online. In magazines. But I just couldn't find the right replacement. And eventually, the abundance of other details that come with transplanting your entire life across an ocean to live on a tiny island took over.

Somewhere between "You'll likely never get pregnant on your own" and the stoplight at "Your best friend has end-stage cancer," I found the website.

Rather, the website found me, in that serendipitous kind of way. Or maybe it's serendipitous if you don't believe in sovereignty. It was sovereignly-serendipitous and it found me weary and wary and worn out and chipped away. I felt forgotten, left behind in a world where every one of my friends was a mom. But more than anything else, I felt forgotten by God. I'd been left dangling with legs swinging to and fro and my prayer-voice echoing off the walls and a bucket hanging motionless in my dugout well, just waiting for someone to come along and make use of it.

Surely the Lord is in this place, this mess, this heartache, and I just can't see it.

"Surely there is a mine for silver," Job said (Job 28:1). *Surely there is a point to all of this,* I sputtered. *Surely the Lord is in this place, this mess, this heartache, and I just can't see it.*

And then I found that website, and with it a curated collection of a lot of other people's tools that were laid out and ready to use. I began to learn how to use parsing and syntax and tense and voice to look past the familiar stories, lifting off layers and mystery and tucking back a corner of the tabernacle-curtain to catch a glimpse into the Holy of Holies. To see a flicker of His presence.

Surely God is in this place.

I had always known the importance of a quiet time. But I was newly discovering the vital importance of quiet-time studying. Paul, however, knew it well. And he gave one imperative, loud, and clear instruction on the matter to Timothy in his second letter:

> Study and be eager and do your utmost to present yourself to God approved (tested by trial), a workman who has no cause to be ashamed, correctly analyzing and accurately dividing [rightly handling and skillfully teaching] the Word of Truth (2 Timothy 2:15 AMPC).

Paul makes use of one particularly interesting phrase here, driving the point of digging deep home: *accurately dividing*. The Greek word is *orthotomeō* and it's a compound of two other words—*orthos* and *tomos*—with a literal meaning of "to make a straight, sharp cut." But there's one much more specific word picture that's buried a little bit deeper in the pages of a Greek lexicon: "to cut new veins in mining."

Interesting, I thought and did a little bit of research. As it turns out, the Roman empire had a rich mining history, and one of the techniques they used was deep-vein mining. It was difficult and dangerous work, with the constant threat of a roof giving way and crushing the men inside. The work was so delicate and so dangerous that only those valuable veins of gold and silver tucked away deep in the earth were profitable enough to justify the risk.

Right there in his letter, Paul tells Timothy to cut straight into God's Word. To cut straight and sharp and deep in order to mine out that gold. Because, as he says in 2 Corinthians 4:8, you might be hard-pressed on every side inside that intricate mine vein. *But you won't be crushed.*

You might be perplexed. *But you won't be in despair.*

You might be persecuted. *But you won't be forgotten.*

You might be thrown down. *But you won't be thrown out.*

Go in, he says, so that the life of Jesus might be manifested in you. Just like God was manifested to Jacob in that Genesis 28 dream when he woke up with a jolt and the words tumbled out of his mouth: "Surely God is in this place, and I did not know it," he said.

Only this time? It's a "Surely the Lord is in this place and I *do* know it" kind of experience.

WE ARE ABOUT to get into the heart of my well. The one that was dug out deep while training my eyes to search for those treasures of darkness that God promises in Isaiah 45:3. The ones that are "hidden riches in secret places, that you may know that I, the Lord, Who call you by your name, am the God of Israel." The ones that are only found in the darkest places.

Blue Letter Bible (blueletterbible.org) is my very favorite online resource. It is, by far, the most powerful, one-stop Scripture study resource I've encountered. It will change the way you study the Bible.

Right there in his letter, Paul tells Timothy to cut straight into God's Word.

With the sheer amount of information available at your fingertips, the website can be a little bit overwhelming at first. But we're going to walk through it together, starting in the New Testament and, step-by-step, exploring the must-know nuances of the Greek language.

It's important to note that I am by no means an expert on the ancient languages. But, by using these resources, I have taught myself enough of the basics to get deeper into the heart of God's Word.

And I haven't looked back.

START BY SEARCHING

Since we just finished talking about Paul's letter to Timothy, let's start there as an example. You can go to the Blue Letter Bible website at www.blueletterbible.org and search for "2 Timothy 2:15" to follow along with me.

When you search for the verse, the results will display half a dozen tools. *Interlinear* is the first tool in the drop-down menu of tools, and it is where I spend most of my time. It's also where we will focus most of this how-to section.

1. Interlinear helps you dissect the elements of a Greek or Hebrew word. This tool opens a variety of resources that take you deeper into the original language, including pronunciation, dictionary aids, outline of biblical usage, Strong's concordance, a lexicon, and more. When you click on the "Interlinear" link, you will see a table of the chosen verse with each word or phrase isolated on its own line along with the following tools:

- The English word, which is linked to a word search that shows the number of times the word is used in a particular translation.
- Strong's concordance, which includes dictionary tools, the outline of biblical usage, and Thayer's Greek Lexicon in addition to concordance results.
- The Greek root of the word and transliteration.
- The Greek pronunciation of the word (click on the audio icon).
- Parsing information, which allows you to identify the particular form of the verb that is being used.

2. **Bibles** presents more than a dozen translations of the selected verse, allowing comparison and prompting better understanding of the author's intent.

3. **Cross-refs** contains the Treasury of Scripture Knowledge Bible Concordance, containing the most exhaustive list of biblical cross-references available.

4. **Commentaries** holds a collection of complete text commentaries, full-length audio sermons from a number of respected pastors and teachers, and other pertinent study resources.

5. **Dictionaries** displays a number of links to entries related to your selected verse in several dictionaries, encyclopedias, topical works, and thematic guides.

6. **Miscellaneous** collects maps, images, and music that correlate to the selected verse.

Before we really start digging into 2 Timothy 2:15, we first need to look at the difference between a concordance and a lexicon. Both are included under the "Strong's" link for a word or phrase in the Interlinear tab. However, that tool actually organizes about half a dozen resources onto one easy-to-access page and isn't limited strictly to the Strong's concordance.

EXHAUSTIVE CONCORDANCES

Strong's concordance is one of the most popular exhaustive concordances among students of the Bible. It not only indexes every single instance of the word you are searching for in Scripture, but it provides several words of the verse's context for a quick assessment of its use in the KJV.

If you were to look at a print version of the concordance, you would see that the book is organized in English alphabetical order and assigns a unique alphanumeric code to each word. That code is detailed in a separate section of the concordance, showing the definition of the word as well as its range of translations and the number of times each translation is used in Scripture.

EXPOSITORY DICTIONARIES

Taking definitions further than the concordance, expository dictionaries help to give an even fuller understanding of a word. They are especially useful for those of us who have little or no formal training in the original biblical languages.

Vine's Complete Expository Dictionary of Old and New Testament Words is included under the "Strong's" link and is a resource that helps to open up the treasures of truth that often lie buried in the original language, sometimes close to the surface and sometimes imbedded far beneath it.

LEXICONS

Following the same alphanumeric coding as the Strong's concordance, a lexicon looks at a thesaurus, the word's root, and its derivatives to convert the vocabulary of the ancient text to vocabulary that is compatible with today's language.

BEFORE YOU DO ANYTHING ELSE,
TAKE NOTE OF THE PARSING

<table>
<tr><td colspan="2">Parsing Information</td></tr>
<tr><td>σπουδάζω</td><td>spoudazō</td></tr>
</table>

Tense: Aorist

Voice: Active

Mood: Imperative

* The Aorist Active Imperative verb form occurs 375 times in the New Testament.

Some Greek verbs can have *hundreds* of different forms. When you see the parse button next to a word in the Interlinear table, it's basically telling you: "Hey, there are a few different veins you could follow on this. Let's get you digging in the right direction."

In parsing the Greek, you need to be aware of three elements: tense, voice, and mood.

TENSE

The tense of a verb describes the place in time that the action occurs. In the most simplistic of terms, it is grouped into three categories: past, present, and future.

Aorist: The verb is considered without regard for past, present, or future time. There isn't really an English equivalent, and aorist verbs are generally rendered in past tense. In this case, the word *study* in 2 Timothy 2:15 is in the aorist tense. The subject is the doer of the action, and it's an absolute command.

Present: In the present tense, verbs show a continuous action that is in progress and happening in real time.

Future: This tense indicates the very certain occurrence of an event which has not yet transpired.

Perfect (both past and present): This tense describes an action that has been completed in the past, the results of which are still continuing in the present in full effect so that the action does not need to be repeated.

Imperfect (past): Similar to the present tense, the imperfect is a continuous action, but it indicates one that repeatedly happened for some extended period of time in the past.

VOICE

The voice indicates who the subject is in relation to the action.

Active: The subject is the doer or performer of the action.

Passive: The subject is the recipient of the action.

Middle: The subject is acting in his own interest, or on his own behalf upon himself.

MOOD

A verb's mood indicates whether the asserted statement is fact or if there is only the possibility of its actual occurrence.

Indicative: A simple statement of fact that an action occurs, has occurred, or will occur.

Imperative: An absolute command that requires full obedience by the hearer.

Subjunctive: Indicates that an action is possible or potential, and may or may not occur (depending upon the circumstances).

Optative: Also indicates a possible or potential action, but it is more of a wish or a hope for an action to occur.

Participle: Turns the verb into an adjective by adding an –ing or –ed to it.

Infinitive: Turns the verb into the subject of a sentence by adding *to* in front of it.

❶ THE ROOT WORD

> Study to shew thyself approved unto God, a workman that needeth not to
> be ashamed, rightly dividing the word of truth.

You might be surprised to learn that where other translations begin 2 Timothy 2:15 with words like *endeavor*, *be diligent*, or even *do your best*, the King James Version simply uses the word *study* (above). I wondered why that particular word was chosen until I went to the Interlinear tab, then to the Strong's link for *study* (G4704), and clicked on the root word.

Sometimes I follow those root word links all the way back until there is nowhere left to go, just to see what they have to say. Sort of like tracing one branch of a tree all the way down its trunk and into the earth. In this case, the root-trail went back four words deep and stopped at the word *pous*—it means "foot" or "footstool"; "disciples listening to their teacher's instruction are said to be at his feet." So, you can make the connection back to *spoudazo* as "studying at the feet of a teacher."

σπουδάζω

Transliteration	Pronunciation
spoudazo	*spü-dä'-zō*

Part of Speech	Root Word (Etymology)
verb	From σπουδή (G4710)

Dictionary Aids

Vine's Expository Dictionary: View Entry
TDNT Reference: 7:559,1069

KJV Translation Count - Total: 11x

The KJV translates Strong's G4704 in the following manner: endeavour (3x), do diligence (2x), be diligent (2x), give diligence (1x), be forward (1x), labour (1x), study (1x).

Outline of Biblical Usage

    I. to hasten, make haste
    II. to exert one's self, endeavour, give diligence

Strong's Definitions

σπουδάζω **spoudázō**, spoo-dad'-zo; from G4710; to use speed, i.e. to make effort, be prompt or earnest:—do (give) diligence, be diligent (forward), endeavour, labour, study.

Thayer's Greek Lexicon

σπουδάζω; future σπουδάσω (a later form for the early -άσομαι, cf. Krüger, § 40, s. v., vol. i, p. 190; B. 53 (46); [W., 89 (85); Veitch, s.v.]); 1 aor. ἐσπούδασα; (σπουδή, q.v.); from Soph. and Arstph. down;   a. *to hasten, make haste*: foll. by an inf. (cf. σπεύδω, 1), 2 Tim. iv. 9, 21; Tit iii.12 [al. refer these exx. to b. ; but cf. Holtzmann, Com. on 2 Tim. 2:15].   b. *to exert oneself, endeavor, give difference*: foll. by an inf., Gal ii:10; Eph iv: 3; 1 Th. ii: 17; 2 Tim ii:15; Heb. iv:11; 2 Peter 1:10; 2 Pet i. 10; iii. 14; foll. by an acc. with an inf 2 Pet i:15.*

The Strong's entry for the word "study" used in 2 Timothy 2:15.

If you look up the cross-references listed in the Thayer's Greek Lexicon for *pous*, you will see the mention of Mary, who sat at Jesus' feet and heard His word while her sister busied and distracted herself with other things (Luke 10:39).

You will read of Paul, who explained his authority to an army captain while being dragged out of the temple—that he was educated under a teacher of the law who was highly respected among all the people (Acts 22:3).

And then there's the man who was called Legion because of the sheer number of demons who lived within his mind—the ones Jesus cast into a herd of pigs. Afterward, that man sat at the feet of Jesus, clothed and in his right mind (Luke 8:35).

Just from tracing the root trails, you now have a three-part explanation of the heart of Paul's command that would have otherwise gone unnoticed: Mary and Legion who sat at the feet of Jesus, and Paul who sat at the feet of a highly respected teacher.

⑪ THAYER'S GREEK LEXICON

The Strong's concordance alphabetically indexes the location of each word in the Bible and provides the word's definition. But lexicons give much more detailed descriptions, and they can be helpful in digging even deeper into the word picture that the author was originally trying to convey.

Because some words can have dozens of different translations, lexicons can have lengthier descriptions. Reading through them might feel a little bit like searching for a needle in a haystack. In those cases, I scan the entry for the reference to the verse I'm studying first and, if it's listed, note the definition that is immediately before or after it.

For our example in 2 Timothy 2:15, Paul's instruction to *show yourself* means *to show quality*. The kind of quality that is publicly displayed for all to see and easily examined with a cursory glance.

OUTLINE OF BIBLICAL USAGE

This tool combines multiple sources (including Strong's concordance and Thayer's Lexicon) for the truest rendering of a word's meaning. In our example, it also provides important cultural context.

We've already looked at the words *study* and *show* in 2 Timothy 2:15. Now let's look at the word *approved* using the Outline of Biblical Usage. If you click on the Strong's link for the word in the Interlinear tab, you will see two definitions:

1. accepted, particularly of coins
2. accepted, pleasing, acceptable

Fairly straightforward, right? But this tool happens to include an important explanation of the definition that specifically references coins:

> In the ancient world there was no banking system as we know it today, and no paper money. All money was made from metal, heated until liquid, poured into moulds and allowed to cool. When the coins were cooled, it was necessary to smooth off the uneven edges. The coins were comparatively soft, and of course many people shaved them closely. In one century, more than eighty laws were passed in Athens to stop the practice of whittling down the coins then in circulation. But some money-changers were men of integrity, who would accept no counterfeit money; they were men of honour who put only genuine, full-weight money into circulation. Such men were called *dokimos*, and this word is used here for the Christian as he is to be seen by the world.[1]

With that description in mind, we now have a much clearer idea of what it means to show ourselves approved before God. We are to be genuine and "rightly weighted"—not whittling things down, taking shortcuts or the easy way out. To stand approved before God is to be the real, quality deal that He can recognize a mile away.

THE PRESENT ACTIVE PARTICIPLE

Let's skip ahead to one last phrase toward the end of 2 Timothy 2:15—one we've referenced at length already: *rightly dividing*. But this time, we're going to go back to that all-important starting point: the parsing.

Tense: present

Voice: active

Mood: participle

The present active participle is one of the most profound verb couplings in the New Testament. It implies an action that the people of God first did *then* and we keep doing *today*. It's a continuous action that is shown in progress and happening in real time, with the subject as the doer or the performer of the action.

As Beth Moore explains it, "When you see a present active participle Greek verb, you can think of the word *continually* preceding the verb."[2] In our example, that means presently, actively, and continually dividing the word of truth the right way. In perpetuity.

The perfect example of a present active participle in action (no pun intended) can be found in Matthew 7:

Ask *and keep asking.*

Seek *and keep seeking.*

Knock *and keep knocking.*

Now that you know the right parsing for the phrase *rightly dividing*, you can take every piece of information provided in the Strong's tools on Blue Letter Bible and form this complete word picture:

Continually cut straight ways in the Word. Make them straight and smooth and handle those cut parts rightly—teaching the truth both directly and correctly. Dissect it and keep dissecting it. Divide it and keep dividing it, cutting new mine veins into it, seeing something new and introducing new things to the same familiar stories.

CHAPTER *six*

Deep Sea Singing

Our entire house was packed up the week before boarding a one-way flight to Maui. Ten years of life and marriage and memories were neatly sorted and labeled and boxed away in a single twenty-foot storage unit.

I managed to find a moment alone on that last day, just before we left our high-desert home. Downstairs, friends scurried around gathering all the misfit odds and ends and sweeping out years of dust and memories. Upstairs, I walked down the hallway to the empty extra bedroom in the back of the house that was always supposed to be the baby's room. Leaning on the wall of the otherwise ordinary room, the weight of its never-met potential sat heavy on my chest.

A movie reel of what could have been played in my mind as I slid to the floor and allowed my mind to dream of the room that I never allowed myself to plan.

The crib would have gone there, I thought, imagining a babe playing on the floor in the beautiful morning light. *And the rocking chair would have been there, in the corner.* I imagined the tiny hangers holding those fit-for-a-minute clothes and the stack of board books for nighttime routines, and I wondered how tattered the favorite blanket might have gotten.

I sat there for a while, until I found that fine line between acknowledging the pain and indulging in it. And then I stood up. And I wiped the tears. And I breathed a deep breath. And I stepped out of the room, closing the door for the last time on that deeply-rooted dream.

A few hours later, we drove away.

Josh went ahead in the moving truck and I followed behind. He led me like that, out of the land of high desert and sagebrush and juniper that had been the landscape of our entire marriage, and into new horizons.

Dreamy, warm, and tropical ones.

TWENTY DAYS INTO our brand-new zip code, a girlfriend sent me a text. We had only known each other a short while, and at the time we'd met, that kitchen table map was just partially colored in black. Our final destination was still very much up in the air, and I had shared our eclectic shortlist with her over dinner.

"Don't ask me why," she wrote in her text, "but do you own a red bathing suit? Specifically a two-piece?"

My curiosity was piqued. I hadn't really talked about that red bikini hunt in any kind of public format that she would have seen. I mean, it was just a bathing suit.

Maybe she saw the photo of us on the dock, I thought—it had been my Facebook cover photo for quite a while.

"Well," I replied, "I used to have one that I loved and wore out, and I've been on the hunt for a new one. But I haven't been able to find the right replacement." Then I asked the very thing she told me not to: "Why?"

"When we met," she wrote back, "you were sharing your story about moving but you couldn't decide between Portland or San Diego or Maui or Atlanta, and we laughed about how extremely different they all were. That night, I saw you. In Maui. On the beach. Very pregnant. In a red two-piece bathing suit. So I have sort of known you were moving to Maui all along. And I have a feeling that you knew you would end up there too.

"But I know that's just the beginning of the promise," she continued. "I know because I don't see stuff like that all the time. So, for what it's worth, I'm praying for your desires to be fulfilled. And I see the picture again every time I hear from you."

Chills rushed over my skin. I flashed back to that last morning in our desert home— I'd woken up to an empty bed and a harried husband who was trying to get through the last-minute checklist that comes with moving your entire life across the ocean. I lay there on the mattress, on the floor of our otherwise empty bedroom, swallowing down sleep and emotion and asking God for a sign that He was in this—in the decision to move, in the continuing choice to do nothing but wait and believe Him for our family—in all of it.

Oh Lord, I prayed, *give us a tangible sign that we are headed in the right direction.*

I thought about the priests in Joshua 3, who were well on their way to crossing the river and walking waist-deep in the Jordan before God stopped the flow of it twenty miles upstream. They had to bravely and boldly walk out into the river first, and then stand there and wait for the path to clear. They didn't know that God would dam up that river twenty miles upstream from where they stood. They just knew that the waters would be cut off. And they moved out and trusted that He would do something to clear the way for them eventually. *Because He said He would.*

> *They had to bravely and boldly walk out into the river first, and then stand there and wait for the path to clear.*

We were already waist-deep in our move, and maybe it was too late to ask.

But I asked anyway.

Twenty days downstream from our move, He had given His sign.

And it was in the form of a red bikini.

FROM THE MOMENT we arrived on Maui, it seemed that God began speaking louder in those morning quiet times. He spoke through exclamatory statements (have you ever noticed the Bible promises marked with exclamation points?) and repeated words and brand-new insights into familiar Bible stories. It was as if the amplification of His voice was in direct proportion to the crescendo of my *how much longer* cries. I swung wildly between the awestruck anticipation of our pending miracle and that familiar white-knuckle faith that left me red-eyed and reeling.

What happens when the miracle doesn't come?

God had been healing my broken heart and binding up the wounds in that Psalm 147:3 way that He has about Him—the one that promises to "heal the brokenhearted and bind up their wounds" (ESV). But the hole in our family remained, gaping and raw, and sometimes feeling like it was ready to swallow me whole.

What happens when the answer doesn't come? I prayed the words honest one morning. It had been nine years since Josh and I had whispered in the dark, dreaming of our family for the very first time. I had been studying the story of Lazarus in John 11—specifically, the part where Jesus tells Martha to roll away the stone in front of Lazarus's grave. And something in that story made my praying-words take a turn, becoming a sort of self-discipleship, preaching to my own soul.

> *What happens when the miracle doesn't come? When you roll away the stone and, with it, all the self-protection and defense mechanisms that have been shielding you from the crushing-blow-possibility of an unanswered prayer? What happens when the stone is rolled and He still hasn't come?*

> *What happens when you tell yourself again that* He will do this—*when you strain your eyes to see into the cave-grave darkness, looking for the tiniest flutter of life, the smallest hint of a miracle, and all you see is nothing?*

> *What happens when your arms are shaking, blood-drained and strength-sapped from holding them up like Moses did that time that God told him that as long as he kept his arms up the Israelites would win that battle, and the second he dropped them, they would start losing? What happens when your faith is punctured through, and God asks you to remain still and full of holes?*

To be caught believing still.

To keep trusting still.

To remind yourself that He is good still, in that stillness of remaining.

It is nothing for you! *I want to scream and drop my hands and ball my fists and pound frustration on holy robes. Because I don't understand any of it.*

"Moses' hands became heavy." It says it right there in Exodus 17:12. "So they took a stone and put it under him, and he sat on it." Jesus told Martha to roll away the stone in immediate anticipation of the miracle. Aaron and Hur rolled the stone over in anticipation of a miraculous, this-could-take-awhile victory. Moses didn't know how long he would have to sit there like that, but he sat...in an excruciating wait for victory.

And so...I will start over again. I will study these verses anew. And sit here with You. And dwell. And remain. And abide with You.

And wait for Your miracle.

NOT LONG AFTER that, I sat in bed on another morning for another quiet time, and I was filled again with a certain amount of anxiety. I was suddenly fearful that we had been praying the wrong way for all those years. Believing God for the wrong thing. Looking for Him in the wrong direction.

I was terrified that I would look up one day and realize that God was standing on the entire other side of a gaping-mouthed canyon, waving His arms wildly to get my attention. Then cupping holy hands around His merciful mouth to yell, "Hey! I'm over here! That's not Me! That voice You're listening to is not Mine!" I was afraid of that childhood feeling of burying your face in Dad's legs, squeezing tight to the safety of him, before looking up and realizing that you're clinging to a stranger instead.

And out of that anxiety and fear came three simple prayer-words: *confirm or deny.*

I had been praying for days, with words bold and brave and marked with a confident understanding that His promised pregnancy would happen soon. But that morning I was suddenly embarrassed about it. For praying that way—still, after all this time.

I begged Him to affirm that I was, in fact, hearing from Him. That I was not crazy or confusing His voice or twisting His Word into something I desperately wanted to hear.

Oh Lord, meet me here, I prayed. *Confirm or deny.*

> *I begged Him to affirm that I was, in fact, hearing from Him.*

TWO HOURS LATER, I was sitting at my desk when a new email notification popped up in the corner of my screen. It was from a woman I had recently hired to manage my social media accounts. She was purely a business connection, and she was entirely uninvolved in our story.

She was working on cultivating a Pinterest board called *The Life I Love* from a brain-dump email I had sent a week earlier. I'd given her a list of my favorite things, and she wanted my opinion about a pin she was considering adding.

"Random question of the day!" she wrote. "How do you feel about this red bikini?"

LATER THAT SUMMER, I sat next to a girlfriend on the beach in the heat of summer. The south swell was in full effect, creating a massive shore break of waves that locals call double-overhead high. Some were as high as 12 feet.

We sat a safe distance away, with an umbrella shielding us from the tropical sun, and we watched the dwarfed shadows of our husbands bodysurfing in the break.

"I floated out here last winter," she told me. The winter-calm waves had been still, the sea glassy. "My ears were just below the surface of the water, and I listened to the whales singing so loud and so clear that everything inside of me vibrated."

I never really stopped to think that you could just poke your head underwater to hear the whales sing. But it turns out you can. Those whale songs can carry on under the water for miles. Every single year, humpbacks leave the frigid Alaskan water to make their yearly winter migration through our warm tropical sea to have their babies—December to May, just like clockwork.

And they come singing their way through the winter.

I tried to hear them a couple of times, but I never could manage to catch the whales in their song. Many winter beach days would find me wading out, floating, and listening to silence.

Wade. Float. Listen.

Still nothing.

Wade. Float. Listen.

Over and over and over again. But still, no matter how many times I tried, I never heard them.

Until one day when Josh went out into the water with me. Only he went out a little bit deeper than I had been going. I had always stayed close to the shore, where toes could still touch and feet could still stand, safe and comfortable.

He went under the water and quickly came back up with a sparkle in his eye.

"You can hear them," he said.

So I swam out to where he was and went underwater right where he did. And then I came back up, frustrated, shaking my head.

"Dive down all the way to the bottom," he said. "Hover right above the surface of the sand, and listen. You'll hear them."

So I took a deeper breath than the last and dove down under the water and fought to stay down and strained my ears when, finally, I heard it.

It was faint. They were far, but I heard it. A faint whisper of a whale song.

I was fascinated that something far enough away to be entirely out of sight could still be heard under the water. I read a *National Geographic* article one time that said those deep vibrations can even travel for thousands of underwater miles.[1] If a whale song can make that kind of breadth, it can also travel to equal depth—reaching miles below where that whale swims.

All the way down into the most secret recesses of the sea.

MOSES WAS OVERWHELMED with the responsibility of shepherding an entire nation of stubborn people.

It was time to move them out of the temporary home they had settled into at the base of Mount Sinai and lead them into the Promised Land—a vast expanse of terrain that was already occupied by foreign people with large and powerful armies.

After begging for confirmation that God was, in fact, leading them into Operation Take the Land I Have for You, Moses asked for one more sign that God was with them:

"Show me Your glory," he whispered toward the end of Exodus 33.

"Okay," God replied. "I'll show you My glory by making all of My goodness pass before you, and I will proclaim the name of the Lord before you" (vv. 18-19, my paraphrase).

Did you catch that last part? The part about God proclaiming His name over Moses as He passed His glory-goodness over? It sat there, tucked into the middle of verse 19 all this time, and I had never noticed it before.

I knew how Moses felt. I'd felt it before—wanting so badly to see God's glory. But I never noticed that part of the glory-revelation is God proclaiming His name as He goes by.

After being safely hidden away in a dug-out hole inside a rock, God covered Moses with His hand. And only then, when he was hidden away in the darkness of that dug-out rock, under the shadow of God's hand, did He pass by, proclaiming His name.

We can borrow Zephaniah's words to help narrate the moment:

> The LORD your God in your midst, the Mighty One, will save; He will rejoice over you with gladness, He will quiet you with His love, He will rejoice over you with singing (Zephaniah 3:17).

And the word for God's singing-voice? It also means "to proclaim."

His song is the same in the dug-out rock as it is in the deepest parts of the sea. You can dive down into the depths of His Word and dig down deep into the carved-out depths of His presence, and you can strain your ears to hear His still, small whisper-voice. And eventually, you'll hear Him. Rejoicing over you with singing and proclaiming His name over you.

After being safely hidden away in a dug-out hole inside a rock, God covered Moses with His hand.

And that's right about the time that you join in on the song and sing His name right back to Him, right there in the depths.

While we're on the topic of depth, there is one more thing I want us to look at together. Tucked into the middle of the book of Job, a cynical friend asks a rhetorical question. "Can you search out the deep things of God?" Zophar asks. "Can you find out the limits of the Almighty?"

And this, dear friends, is where we will start to dig.

BIBLICAL HEBREW

is primarily a language of verbs that are derived from roots.
A verbal stem is an offshoot of the root that is used to indicate
the properties of voice and aspect.

English (KJV)		Strong's	Root Form (Hebrew)		Parsing	
Canst thou by searching	PHR	H2714	חֵקֶר	cheqer	◁))	
find out	PHR	H4672	מָצָא	'matsa'	◁))	PARSE
God	PHR	H433	אֱלוֹהַּ	'elowahh	◁))	
canst thou find	PHR	H4672	מָצָא	matsa'	◁))	PARSE
out the Almighty	PHR	H7706	שַׁדַּי	Shadday	◁))	
unto perfection	PHR	H8503	תַּכְלִית	takliyth	◁))	

Parsing Information

מָצָא   matsa'

Stem: Qal

Aspect: Infinitive

STEM

Qal – simple action, active voice

Niphal – simple action, passive voice

Piel – intensive action, active voice

Pual – intensive action, passive voice

Hiphil – causal action, active voice

Hophal – causal action, passive voice

Hithpael – intensive action, middle voice

ASPECT

Perfect – a simple, completed action

Imperfect – an incomplete action

Cohortative – a first-person command

Imperative – a second-person command

Jussive – a third-person command

Participle – an active and continuous action

CANST THOU BY SEARCHING

חקר *cheqer*

STRONG'S H2714

Root Word (Etymology): H2713

chaqar, *khaw-kar'; a primitive root; properly, to penetrate; hence, to examine intimately:—find out, (make) search (out), seek (out), sound, try.*

Gesenius' Hebrew-Chaldee Lexicon:

The primary idea is perhaps that of searching in the earth by digging.

The KJV translates Strong's H2714 in the following manner:

search (6x), unsearchable (2x), unsearchable (with H369) (1x), finding out (1x), without number (1x), search out (1x).

Gesenius' Hebrew-Chaldee Lexicon:

that which is known by investigation, hidden, secret. Job 38:16, "the most secret recesses of the sea." Metaph. Job 11:7.

FIND OUT

מצא *matsa'*

STRONG'S H4672

Parsing Information:

Stem: *Qal*

Aspect: *Imperfect*

Outline of Biblical Usage:

I. to find, attain to
  A. (Qal)
    i. to find
      a. to find, secure, acquire, get
      b. to find (what is lost)
      c. to meet, encounter
      d. to find (a condition)
      e. to learn, devise

Gesenius' Hebrew-Chaldee Lexicon:

to come to, i.e. to attain to, to arrive at anything, followed by Job 11:7, hence *to obtain, to acquire, to receive.* Gen. 26:12, "Isaac in that year received a hundred measures," ... So *to obtain* knowledge, Pro. 3:13; 8:9.

GOD

אֱלוֹהַּ *'elowahh*

STRONG'S H433

Strong's Definitions:

elôwahh, el-o'-ah; rarely (shortened) elôahh; probably prolonged (emphatic) from H410; a deity or the Deity:—God, god.

Gesenius' Hebrew-Chaldee Lexicon:

(1) of *any god*, Dan. 11:37-39; 2 Chr. 32:15; Neh. 9:17.

(2) mostly *of the true God*, Deu. 32:15; Ps. 50:22, and forty times in the book of Job.

(A) in a plural sense – (1) of *gods* or *deities* in general, whether true or false. "the gods of the Egyptians," Exodus 12:12. "strange gods," Gen. 35:2, 4; Deu. 29:18. "new gods," Deu. 32:17. Sometimes, from the more common popular usage, Jehovah and idols are comprehended under this common name; Ps. 86:8, "there is none like unto thee among the gods, O Jehovah!" Ex. 18:11; 22:19. Elsewhere the idea of divinity...is attributed to Jehovah alone. Isa. 44:6.

UNTO PERFECTION

תַּכְלִית *takliyth*

STRONG'S H8503

Outline of Biblical Usage:

I. end, perfection, consummation, completion, completeness

    A. end
    B. completeness

Strong's Definitions:

taklîyth, tak-leeth'; from H3615; completion; by implication, an extremity:—end, perfect(-ion).

Gesenius' Hebrew-Chaldee Lexicon:

(1) *perfection, completion*, Job 11:7.

(2) *extremity, end, conclusion*. Neh. 3:21. Job 26:10, "as far as where light ends in darkness." Job 28:3, "as far as all the extremity (in the most profound recesses of the earth) search is made."

FIND THE TRAIL MARKERS

It had been a year of Maui sunsets when God started speaking the words. The too-good-to-be-true kinds of words that indicated the earliest signs of an upcoming miracle.

Womb. Watch. Wait.

It was around Easter that they first began stirring. In the four days that led up to the holiday, three girlfriends gave birth to four babies, and five other girlfriends shared news of their pregnancies.

That Friday, I cried alone in the dark, stuck in my own Good Friday story of death and loss, waiting for my Resurrection Sunday.

How much longer?! I scribbled the words bold in my prayer journal a few weeks later. It was getting increasingly difficult to remain still and wait when I was antsy to run ahead and make things happen.

Womb: You will birth a child.

Watch: Keep your eyes locked on the horizon line. Your miracle is as sure as the sunrise.

Wait: Though it tarries, wait, because it will surely come (Habakkuk 2:3).

For four months, those three words showed up everywhere. Consistently. Almost infuriatingly. Whether it was in a verse that was part of my quiet time or dug up in a word study or tucked away in a cross-reference or mentioned in a photo caption on social media. He repeated His promise. Over and over again.

But I thought I was making it all up. I thought that I was so desperate to hear those specific words that I was actually looking for them. Subconsciously scanning and scouring and searching until I found what I was looking for.

I was afraid that I had started twisting Scripture to fit what I wanted God to say.

I was afraid that I had started twisting Scripture to fit what I *wanted* God to say.

So I stopped digging. Stopped journaling. Stopped keeping my eyes peeled for the smallest reflective treasure-surface. I was exhausted with the wait and confused by the endless womb-watch-wait references.

Eventually, I stopped reading my Bible altogether. Two weeks went by without my even opening it. I was hoping for a fresh perspective—to put a stop to the near obsession I had in tracking those three repeated words. I thought that in taking a break, I would reset God's voice and retune the melody of His song over me.

It was a Tuesday morning when I finally decided enough time had gone by and I picked up where He and I had left off. With a deep breath, I pulled the ribbon bookmark that opened my Bible to Nehemiah 9, and I began to read.

The Israelites had gotten off track. They refused to obey God's commands or remember the miracles He had performed in their slavery-redemption. They had sinned in so many ways.

> ## "In His manifold mercies He did not forsake them."

"But You are God," Nehemiah said in verse 17. "Ready to pardon, gracious and merciful, slow to anger, and abundant in kindness."

And then these two brown eyes laid onto a two-word phrase that stopped me in my quiet-time tracks: "In His *manifold mercies* He did not forsake them" (Nehemiah 9:19, my paraphrase).

I started to think about those manifold mercies. The ones that are more numerous than the 3442 days I had spent waiting for our family. The ones that are abundant and enough and abundantly enough. The ones that are made up of a million tiny, seemingly inconsequential parts and pieces. But together, they form the trail markers of His mercy.

Then I did what I had deliberately stopped doing for weeks: I dug into His mercy. And

God picked up the conversation where I had abruptly cut it off. When I was tired of following a trail of words I thought that I had created myself, He pounded the trail-marker-post into the dirt. And it sat waiting there for me whenever I was ready to start digging again:

MERCIES
רחם – (1) *womb*, Gen. 49:25

Surely God is in this place.

The moment I clicked on that H2713 link to explore the root of that *canst thou by searching* phrase and saw those lexicon words I knew I was in the right mine-vein. They were right there waiting for me like ribbons tied around stakes with a light breeze moving the loose ends in a gentle hello:

"The primary idea is perhaps that of searching in the earth by digging."

DON'T FORGET THE PARSING

As with the Greek samples in the previous chapter, the parsing for Hebrew words is extremely important.

If you take our example from page 91 and look at the Outline of Biblical Usage for the phrase *find out* on the Blue Letter Bible website, you will see more than 30 different definitions for that one Hebrew word:

I. to find, attain to
  A. (Qal)
    i. to find
      a. to find, secure, acquire, get
        (thing sought)
      b. to find (what is lost)
      c. to meet, encounter
      d. to find (a condition)
      e. to learn, devise
    ii. to find out

      a. to find out
      b. to detect
      c. to guess
    iii. to come upon,
      light upon
      a. to happen upon, meet,
        fall in with
      b. to hit
      c. to befall

B. (Niphal)

  i. to be found

    a. to be encountered, be lighted upon, be discovered

    b. to appear, be recognised

    c. to be discovered, be detected

    d. to be gained, be secured

  ii. to be, be found

    a. to be found in

    b. to be in the possession of

    c. to be found in (a place), happen to be

  d. to be left (after war)

  e. to be present

  f. to prove to be

  g. to be found sufficient, enough

C. (Hiphil)

  i. to cause to find, attain

  ii. to cause to light upon, come upon, come

  iii. to cause to encounter

  iv. to present (offering)

But sometimes even knowing the right parsing can still leave you somewhat confused. In our example, the qal stem includes more than a dozen variations of the same word, and this is where the lexicon is helpful.

You can take what you know about the parsing and look for the corresponding stem in the lexicon. In a lot of cases, the particular verse you're studying is even referenced, enabling you to hone in on the appropriate use of the verb.

Note: The qal stem is the main root of any Hebrew word and, by default, is the top definition in the Gesenius Hebrew-Chaldee Lexicon.

EXPLORE THE REFERENCES

At the end of Zophar's rhetorical question in Job 11:7, he asked if it was possible to find out the limits of God. If you read the verse in the King James Version, you'll see that it translates *the limits* as *all perfection*, and the Hebrew word that's used there is *takliyth*. It refers to the most extreme end of something. The conclusion of it. Following the path as far as it can possibly go before it dead-ends in perfect revelation.

At the end of the lexicon entry for *takliyth*, there are two interesting references. Both fit within our mine-digging theme, but the second (Job 28:3) fits a little bit more closely. So I hopped over to take a closer look, backing up to verse one for context.

I had previously searched for the word *vein* in the Bible without result when I first started writing this book. Then, when God was ready to tie it in, I practically tripped over it. Right there at the very beginning of Job 28 is another KJV deep-vein trail marker, waving its loose ribbon ends in that gentle hello: "Surely there is a vein for the silver, and a place for gold where they mine it" (Job 28:1 KJV).

English (KJV)		Strong's	Root Form (Hebrew)		Parsing
He setteth	PHR	H7760	שׂוּם suwm	◁))	PARSE
an end	PHR	H7093	קֵץ qets	◁))	
to darkness	PHR	H2822	חֹשֶׁךְ choshek	◁))	
and searcheth out	PHR	H2713	חָקַר chaqar	◁))	PARSE
all perfection	PHR	H8503	תַּכְלִית takliyth	◁))	
the stones	PHR	H68	אֶבֶן 'eben	◁))	
of darkness	PHR	H652	אֹפֶל 'ophel	◁))	
and the shadow of death	PHR	H6757	צַלְמָוֶת tsalmaveth	◁))	

❶ AND SEARCHETH OUT

Did you notice the Hebrew word? It's the same as the root word for the "canst thou by searching" phrase in Job 11:7. The one that means "searching the earth by digging." The parsing of the verb reveals it to be an *active participle* aspect, which is the Hebrew version of Greek's *present active participle*. It implies active and continuous searching: dig and keep digging.

❷ ALL PERFECTION

This is where we find the Job 11 connection—this Hebrew word is the same one used at the end of verse seven, and it provides the anchor for the cross-reference.

THE POWER OF FAMILIARITY

I've already written about the power of following the cross-references in the margins of your Bible as well as the ones referenced in your various study tools. As you read and become more familiar with your Bible, you'll start writing your own cross-reference notes in your Bible margins—ones that aren't necessarily listed outrightly. For example, a certain word in an Old Testament verse will trigger a piece of a New Testament verse, carrying on the conversation from Hebrew to Greek and across generations.

The more I dug into *searching out* and *deep recesses of the sea* and thought about Zophar's rhetorical question, the more I thought of Paul's overarching prayer in Ephesians 3. The one that had him on his knees praying for the group of believers in Ephesus.

> I bow my knees before the Father from whom every family in heaven and on earth derives its name, that He would grant you, according to the riches of His glory, to be strengthened with power through His Spirit in the inner man, so that Christ may dwell in your hearts through faith; and that you, being rooted and grounded in love, *may be able to comprehend* with all the saints *what is the breadth and length and height and depth,* and to know the love of Christ *which surpasses knowledge,* that you may be filled up to all the fullness of God (Ephesians 3:14-19 NASB, emphasis mine).

I took pen to paper and began to dig into Paul's words, finding them strikingly interconnected with the words in Job:

> Job says "Can you?" And Paul says "Lord, do it," praying that you may be eminently able to comprehend, lay hold of with your mind, understand, and learn:
>
> What is the breadth: broad and extensive
>
> and length: used in shadowing forth greatness, extent, and number of the blessings received from Christ.
>
> Job says men put an end to darkness and the shadow of death. Paul continues the thought in his prayer—putting an end to the shadow of death by learning the shadow of His greatness.
>
> and depth: of the deep sea! The kind of depth that cannot separate you from the love of God which is in Christ Jesus our Lord.
>
> and height: with the root showing above and beyond.
>
> Of the love of Christ which
>
> passes: (present active participle—continually) transcends, surpasses, and exceeds, with the root showing beyond pouring out of rivers
>
> knowledge: intelligence and understanding

THE SHADOW OF GLORY

Armed with all of this brand-new, dug-up, hard-to-wrap-your-brain-around information, I'm going to take one from Paul's playbook and stop right here in the middle of mine. To bow my knees before our Father and pray for you.

I pray that you would have the strength to dig and to keep digging. To continually search every nook and cranny and recess of your Bible until there is no dark corner left to dig into, no treasure stone left unturned. I pray that you keep digging in Scripture until you are old and gray, that you may be able to learn the broad and expansive depth of the love of Christ. And I pray that you keep digging that you may learn the deep-sea depth of it. Because that breadth and length and deep-sea depth and heaven-height love of Christ continually surpasses and exceeds your intelligence and understanding.

So I pray that you would have the strength to dig and keep digging.

So I pray that you dig and keep digging. Because you cannot reach the depth, breadth, length, or height of Him. But one thing you can count on: When you get down into the no-light-left, deep-sea parts of God? He will meet you there, rejoicing over you with gladness, quieting you with His knowledge-surpassing love, and rejoicing over you with deep-sea singing.

I pray that in those moments, when you breathe out deeply while holding fistfuls of dug-up gold dust from the depth of God's Word, that you can recognize the shift between the ending of that thick and heavy darkness and the beginning of the outer edges of His glory. The kind that only comes with being hidden in the shadow of His hand as He proclaims and sings His name over you.

I pray that you can comprehend that the shadow of death is really the shadowing-forth of His glory. And it's a glory, hallelujah, for all generations to see, forever and ever kind of glory-greatness.

Amen.

CHAPTER *seven*

The Resources

Now that you know the inner workings of my favorite Scripture study resources, it's time to pull it all together in the simple, step-by-step process that I use for my own quiet time. My approach to studying Scripture is about pulling together the elements that will ground your quiet time, eliminating any guesswork. It's important to note that most days I only use bits and pieces of this system. Some days, I use all of it. I encourage you to try it *all* out, find what works for you, and then modify it to create your own unique system!

THE THINGS I CAN'T LIVE WITHOUT

BIBLE: My go-to quiet time Bible is the *Wide Margin Center-Column Reference Edition* published by Thomas Nelson Publishers.

JOURNAL: As you know by now, I am an *avid* prayer journaler. Somewhere along the line, I realized that I could pray more effectively if I journaled. Writing proved to be the most distraction-free way to pray, and it also provided a chronicle of this entire journey. I have a record of all the things I prayed about which, in turn, helped me to recognize more often when prayers were being answered. This also helps me notice word patterns that God is repeating. When the same verse pops up throughout the week in unconnected contexts, or when themes continue for weeks (or even months), I know what to pay attention to and where I should start digging. They become the trail markers.

It's all in one place. Safely shelved for future reference, my journal is a dug-out well of prayer and study for the generations after me to read. Because the point of all this isn't just you learning how to study Scripture better. It's about changing the quiet-time game for the rest of your life and paving the way for your children (and theirs) to do the same.

ER NOTEBOOK: It doesn't really matter which binder you use to store your notes, but I recommend buying one that's large and durable. Having a more durable binder ended up being helpful in the long run for me since it took me ten years to finally finish *Search the Scriptures*!

DIVIDERS: I use a fine-point Sharpie to write each book of the Bible on the write-on tabs in the binder notebook (which I like over the traditional, paper slide-in dividers). Whichever kind you end up choosing, make sure to get enough to cover all 66 books of the Bible.

PENS: I have specific pens for writing in my prayer journal and multicolored smear-proof pens for my Bible that don't bleed through the page.

JANE'S STUDY-SCRIPTURE SYSTEM

1. BEGIN WITH YOUR BIBLE: READ THE PASSAGE.

If I don't already have something specific that I'm studying (like a Bible study I'm participating in or a book I'm reading), or if I am unsure of where to read, I always reach for the *Search the Scriptures* book first. Having a comprehensive list of what to read, whether it's a three-year Bible study course or a one-year Bible reading plan, is a great way to safeguard against the lackadaisical approach of opening up your Bible and reading whatever page happens to fall open that morning.

2. CROSS-REFERENCE: FOLLOW THE TRAIL.

After reading through the day's passage, the first thing I look for in any section of Scripture is a cross-reference. It's always best to let Scripture explain Scripture first (before consulting any other study tool), and it often involves chasing a treasure trail of glory. Cross-referencing is one of the most powerful tools God uses to speak because He's literally placed a trail marker for you to follow. The side trails are rich and powerful and often surprising, writing a sometimes unexpected narrative.

3. BLUE LETTER BIBLE: DEEP-VEIN MINE.

After chasing down the cross-references, there are usually words or phrases that reso-nate with me, intrigue me, or otherwise pique my interest. For example, treasures that we've already looked at like *manifold mercies* or *rightly dividing* all start with simple curi-osity, and I use the Blue Letter Bible website to dig a little bit deeper into the meaning behind the original Hebrew and Greek words.

(Since this part of my study is separate from the guided questions in *Search the Scrip-tures*, I often include the notes from my cross-referencing and deep-vein mining discov-eries in my prayer journal rather than my binder notebook.)

4. SEARCH THE SCRIPTURES: ANSWER THE QUESTIONS.

Once I've thoroughly dug into the passage, I return to *Search the Scriptures* to read the questions and write the answers in my binder notebook. A lot of times, the questions go in a completely different direction than what I have studied, giving even further insight that I likely hadn't even considered. And though there are some explanatory notes, the author keeps them to an absolute minimum.

I also write color-coded notes in the margins of my Bible throughout the entire study process (see pages 120-122 for my color-coding system). I can't emphasize it enough: Writing what you have learned on paper is so important! It not only helps you commit it to memory, it also leaves a written record of your insights for the generations after you to read.

5. UNRAVEL THE KNOTS: READ A COMMENTARY.

If cross-references have been chased, words have been studied, notes have been written, and I still have an unanswered question or want more information on a passage, the last tool I use is a commentary. There are an overwhelming number of them to choose from and I usually reference the ones available on the Blue Letter Bible website (particu-larly the ones written by Jamieson, Fausset, and Brown; and Matthew Henry). I usually just skim through commentaries until I get to a particular verse I'm stuck on or curious about. Because commentaries are so information heavy, they tend to hurt my brain if I read notes on an entire chapter in one sitting. In fact, I can't remember the last time I read the full commentary section on any one chapter of Scripture. I tend to favor them more for informational tidbits than anything else.

6. WRITE IT ALL OUT: USE A PRAYER JOURNAL.

I journal everything. Thoughts. Discoveries. Lightbulb moments. Prayers. It's often difficult to discern where one of those ends and another begins. And there is always a journal open on my desk when I sit down for my morning quiet time.

I often get asked how I know what goes in the binder notebook and what goes in the journal. Generally, the fill-in-the-blank kind of informational answers get put in the notebook. But when things start shifting from information to personal application, and I feel that familiar moving of the Holy Spirit, that's usually when I move over to my journal. I often write things like "see *Search the Scriptures* notes" in my journal to save on transcribing from one to another.

COLOR-CODED BIBLE NOTES

By now you're probably wondering: *How in the world do I organize all of this information?*

I know. I did too.

When I really began getting serious about digging deeply into Scripture, I was gathering information from so many different sources that I needed a way to organize my notes—especially the ones that were written in the margin of my Bible. I had to recognize what were my own thoughts, what were translations from the Amplified Bible, and what were notes from other pastors, speakers, and commentators. I wanted to be able to open to a passage and quickly make sense of the chicken scratch in its margins. So I came up with a color-coding system using a set of rainbow-colored pens, and I assigned a color to each genre of notes.

Here's the breakdown:

—— My Personal Notes

—— Repeated Phrases

—— The Amplified Bible

—— Definitions, Search the Scriptures

—— Cross-References

—— Pastors, Speakers, Commentaries

MY PERSONAL NOTES

The purple ink represents my own thoughts as I read or study. I underline in purple when things strike me, and sometimes I write a short thought or even a date in the margin that points me to a particular journal entry that is especially jaw-dropping. I know that when I see something written in purple, it's an off-the-cuff remark about something that was stirring in my heart, and it was important enough that I wanted to remember it.

REPEATED PHRASES

The more I began digging deeply into my Bible, the more I noticed patterns, especially words or phrases that were repeated within a chapter (or within a couple of chapters). And they were close enough together to stop and take note. I know that all Scripture is God-breathed, so every single sentence has divine weight. When God says something once, it's important. When He says it twice, pay attention—He's emphasizing a point. But when He says it three times (or more)? You'd better stop and take notice.

When I recognize a pattern of repeated words or phrases within a page of each other, I box them out in orange and draw a line to connect the two (or more) together. If the repeated phrase is on the next page, I draw a line to the edge of the page, turn it, and continue the line to the connecting word or phrase. Having them boxed out tells me: "Hey, this is important!"

(Bonus: Repeated phrases also serve as cross-references.)

> Words that are repeated throughout Scripture are repeated because they bear repeating. It's God's way of saying, "Don't let this go in one ear and out the other."[1]—Mark Batterson

THE AMPLIFIED BIBLE

The Amplified Bible does exactly what you might think it does. It "amplifies" the text by adding parenthetical statements to explain the original language more descriptively. I reference the Amplified Bible quite a bit in my studying and often come across more vibrant and detailed versions of verses that I especially love compared to my traditional translation. When that happens, I write the Amplified Bible's translation in my Bible's margin in green ink.

DEFINITIONS, *SEARCH THE SCRIPTURES*

As you know by now, I put a huge emphasis on word definitions while I study. It's why I love the Amplified Bible so much, and it fuels the curiosity that gets me digging daily into the Greek and Hebrew lexicons. I write these notes in black ink, as well as standard English dictionary definitions and poignant explanatory notes from *Search the Scriptures*.

CROSS-REFERENCES

Red ink is the key for a lot of how I study. It's the very first thing I look for in any section of Scripture before digging into word studies or other Scripture-mining tools. As previously mentioned, I always let Scripture explain Scripture before anything else through the use of cross-references. If my Bible includes a marginal reference that especially catches my attention, I circle it in red. If I discover a reference throughout my study time that isn't already cited, I write it in the margin next to the verse in red.

PASTORS, SPEAKERS, COMMENTARIES

When I see a marginal note in blue ink, I know that I'm reading a thought, insight, or quotation from another person (making sure to also note the author for my own reference). Whether it's a pastor, a speaker at a conference, notes from a Bible study, or a commentary I'm reading, blue ink is an indicator to me that the point struck a chord, but I need to follow up on the information to confirm its accuracy.

THE ONE-YEAR BIBLE READING PLAN

The Bible is a big book, and without a strategic plan it is very easy to give up on reading it through before you even finish Genesis. To help, I've adapted a one-year reading plan from the folks over at The Bible Project that pairs a psalm with a daily reading from either the Old or New Testament.

The book of Psalms is possibly my most favorite book of the Bible, and it has also been the prayer book of Jews and Christians for thousands of years. By having a psalm as part of your everyday reading, you not only become intimately familiar with the words, but you'll also have read and prayed through the book of Psalms 2.5 times by the end of the year.

We've made it easy to keep track of your progress, so dog-ear the pages and come back to check the box every day after your quiet time.

January

- [ ] **1** Gen 1-3, Ps 1
- [ ] **2** Gen 4-7, Ps 2
- [ ] **3** Gen 8-11, Ps 3
- [ ] **4** Gen 12-15, Ps 4
- [ ] **5** Gen 16-18, Ps 5
- [ ] **6** Gen 19-21, Ps 6
- [ ] **7** Gen 22-24, Ps 7
- [ ] **8** Gen 25-28, Ps 8
- [ ] **9** Gen 29-31, Ps 9
- [ ] **10** Gen 32-34, Ps 10
- [ ] **11** Gen 35-37, Ps 11
- [ ] **12** Gen 38-40, Ps 12

- [ ] **13** Gen 41-42, Ps 13
- [ ] **14** Gen 43-45, Ps 14
- [ ] **15** Gen 46-47, Ps 15
- [ ] **16** Gen 48-50, Ps 16
- [ ] **17** Ex 1-3, Ps 17
- [ ] **18** Ex 4-6, Ps 18
- [ ] **19** Ex 7-9, Ps 19
- [ ] **20** Ex 10-12, Ps 20
- [ ] **21** Ex 13-15, Ps 21
- [ ] **22** Ex 16-18, Ps 22
- [ ] **23** Ex 19-21, Ps 23
- [ ] **24** Ex 22-24, Ps 24

- [ ] **25** Ex 25-27, Ps 25
- [ ] **26** Ex 28-29, Ps 26
- [ ] **27** Ex 30-31, Ps 27
- [ ] **28** Ex 32-34, Ps 28
- [ ] **29** Ex 35-40, Ps 29
- [ ] **30** Lev 1-4, Ps 30
- [ ] **31** Lev 5-7, Ps 31

February

- [ ] **1** Lev 8-10, Ps 32
- [ ] **2** Lev 11-13, Ps 33
- [ ] **3** Lev 14-15, Ps 34
- [ ] **4** Lev 16-18, Ps 35
- [ ] **5** Lev 19-20, Ps 36
- [ ] **6** Lev 21-23, Ps 37
- [ ] **7** Lev 24-25, Ps 38
- [ ] **8** Lev 26-27, Ps 39
- [ ] **9** Num 1-4, Ps 40
- [ ] **10** Num 5-7, Ps 41
- [ ] **11** Num 8-10, Ps 42
- [ ] **12** Num 11-13, Ps 43
- [ ] **13** Num 14-16, Ps 44
- [ ] **14** Num 17-18, Ps 45
- [ ] **15** Num 19-21, Ps 46
- [ ] **16** Num 22-24, Ps 47
- [ ] **17** Num 25-27, Ps 48
- [ ] **18** Num 28-30, Ps 49
- [ ] **19** Num 31-32, Ps 50
- [ ] **20** Num 33-34, Ps 51
- [ ] **21** Num 35-36, Ps 52
- [ ] **22** Deut 1-3, Ps 53
- [ ] **23** Deut 4-6, Ps 54
- [ ] **24** Deut 7-9, Ps 55
- [ ] **25** Deut 10-12, Ps 56
- [ ] **26** Deut 13-14, Ps 57
- [ ] **27** Deut 15-16, Ps 58
- [ ] **28** Deut 17-20, Ps 59
- [ ] **29** Deut 21-23, Ps 60

March

- [ ] **1** Deut 24-27, Ps 61
- [ ] **2** Deut 28-29, Ps 62
- [ ] **3** Deut 30-31, Ps 63
- [ ] **4** Deut 32-34, Ps 64
- [ ] **5** Josh 1-4, Ps 65
- [ ] **6** Josh 5-8, Ps 66
- [ ] **7** Josh 9-12, Ps 67
- [ ] **8** Josh 13-21, Ps 68
- [ ] **9** Josh 22-24, Ps 69
- [ ] **10** Judg 1-3, Ps 70
- [ ] **11** Judg 4-5, Ps 71
- [ ] **12** Judg 6-8, Ps 72
- [ ] **13** Judg 9-12, Ps 73
- [ ] **14** Judg 13-15, Ps 74
- [ ] **15** Judg 16-18, Ps 75
- [ ] **16** Judg 19-21, Ps 76
- [ ] **17** Ruth, Ps 77
- [ ] **18** 1 Sam 1-3, Ps 78
- [ ] **19** 1 Sam 4-8, Ps 79
- [ ] **20** 1 Sam 9-12, Ps 80
- [ ] **21** 1 Sam 13-14, Ps 81
- [ ] **22** 1 Sam 15-17, Ps 82
- [ ] **23** 1 Sam 18-20, Ps 83
- [ ] **24** 1 Sam 21-24, Ps 84
- [ ] **25** 1 Sam 25-27, Ps 85
- [ ] **26** 1 Sam 28-31, Ps 86
- [ ] **27** 2 Sam 1-3, Ps 87
- [ ] **28** 2 Sam 4-8, Ps 88
- [ ] **29** 2 Sam 9-12, Ps 89
- [ ] **30** 2 Sam 13-15, Ps 90
- [ ] **31** 2 Sam 16-18, Ps 91

April

- [ ] **1** 2 Sam 19-21, Ps 92
- [ ] **2** 2 Sam 22-24, Ps 93
- [ ] **3** 1 Kings 1-3, Ps 94
- [ ] **4** 1 Kings 4-7, Ps 95
- [ ] **5** 1 Kings 8-10, Ps 96
- [ ] **6** 1 Kings 11-13, Ps 97
- [ ] **7** 1 Kings 14-16, Ps 98
- [ ] **8** 1 Kings 17-19, Ps 99
- [ ] **9** 1 Kings 20-22, Ps 100
- [ ] **10** 2 Kings 1-3, Ps 101
- [ ] **11** 2 Kings 4-7, Ps 102

- [ ] **12** 2 Kings 8-11, Ps 103
- [ ] **13** 2 Kings 12-14, Ps 104
- [ ] **14** 2 Kings 15-17, Ps 105
- [ ] **15** 2 Kings 18-19, Ps 106
- [ ] **16** 2 Kings 20-22, Ps 107
- [ ] **17** 2 Kings 23-25, Ps 108
- [ ] **18** Isa 1-4, Ps 109
- [ ] **19** Isa 5-8, Ps 110
- [ ] **20** Isa 9-12, Ps 111
- [ ] **21** Isa 13-17, Ps 112
- [ ] **22** Isa 18-22, Ps 113

- [ ] **23** Isa 23-27, Ps 114
- [ ] **24** Isa 28-30, Ps 115
- [ ] **25** Isa 31-35, Ps 116
- [ ] **26** Isa 36-38, Ps 117
- [ ] **27** Isa 39-41, Ps 118
- [ ] **28** Isa 42-44, Ps 119:1-32
- [ ] **29** Isa 45-48, Ps 119:33-64
- [ ] **30** Isa 49-51, Ps 119:65-96

May

- [ ] **1** Isa 52-54, Ps 119:97-128
- [ ] **2** Isa 55-57, Ps 119:129-152
- [ ] **3** Isa 58-60, Ps 119:153-176
- [ ] **4** Isa 61-64, Ps 120
- [ ] **5** Isa 65-66, Ps 121
- [ ] **6** Hosea 1-5, Ps 122
- [ ] **7** Hosea 6-10, Ps 123
- [ ] **8** Hosea 11-14, Ps 124
- [ ] **9** Joel 1-3, Ps 125

- [ ] **10** Amos 1-5, Ps 126
- [ ] **11** Amos 6-9, Ps 127
- [ ] **12** Obad, Ps 128
- [ ] **13** Jon 1-4, Ps 129
- [ ] **14** Mic 1-4, Ps 130
- [ ] **15** Mic 5-7, Ps 131
- [ ] **16** Nah 1-3, Ps 132
- [ ] **17** Hab 1-3, Ps 133
- [ ] **18** Zeph 1-3, Ps 134
- [ ] **19** Job 1-3, Ps 135
- [ ] **20** Job 4-7, Ps 136

- [ ] **21** Job 8-11, Ps 137
- [ ] **22** Job 12-15, Ps 138
- [ ] **23** Job 16-19, Ps 139
- [ ] **24** Job 20-23, Ps 140
- [ ] **25** Job 24-28, Ps 141
- [ ] **26** Job 29-31, Ps 142
- [ ] **27** Job 32-34, Ps 143
- [ ] **28** Job 35-37, Ps 144
- [ ] **29** Job 38-39, Ps 145
- [ ] **30** Job 40-42, Ps 146
- [ ] **31** Ps 1-2, Ps 147

June

- [ ] **1** Prov 1-3, Ps 148
- [ ] **2** Prov 4-6, Ps 149
- [ ] **3** Prov 7-9, Ps 150
- [ ] **4** Prov 10-12, Ps 1
- [ ] **5** Prov 13-15, Ps 2
- [ ] **6** Prov 16-18, Ps 3
- [ ] **7** Prov 19-21, Ps 4
- [ ] **8** Prov 22-24, Ps 5
- [ ] **9** Prov 25-27, Ps 6
- [ ] **10** Prov 28-31, Ps 7

- [ ] **11** Eccles 1-4, Ps 8
- [ ] **12** Eccles 5-8, Ps 9
- [ ] **13** Eccles 9-12, Ps 10
- [ ] **14** Song of Sol 1-4, Ps 11
- [ ] **15** Song of Sol 5-8, Ps 12
- [ ] **16** Jer 1-3, Ps 13
- [ ] **17** Jer 4-6, Ps 14
- [ ] **18** Jer 7-9, Ps 15
- [ ] **19** Jer 10-13, Ps 16
- [ ] **20** Jer 14-17, Ps 17

- [ ] **21** Jer 18-22, Ps 18
- [ ] **22** Jer 23-25, Ps 19
- [ ] **23** Jer 26-29, Ps 20
- [ ] **24** Jer 30-32, Ps 21
- [ ] **25** Jer 33-36, Ps 22
- [ ] **26** Jer 37-39, Ps 23
- [ ] **27** Jer 40-44, Ps 24
- [ ] **28** Jer 45-48, Ps 25
- [ ] **29** Jer 49-50, Ps 26
- [ ] **30** Jer 51-52, Ps 27

July

- [ ] **1** Lam 1-2, Ps 28
- [ ] **2** Lam 3, Ps 29
- [ ] **3** Lam 4-5, Ps 30
- [ ] **4** Ezek 1-4, Ps 31
- [ ] **5** Ezek 5-8, Ps 32
- [ ] **6** Ezek 9-12, Ps 33
- [ ] **7** Ezek 13-15, Ps 34
- [ ] **8** Ezek 16-18, Ps 35
- [ ] **9** Ezek 19-21, Ps 36
- [ ] **10** Ezek 22-24, Ps 37
- [ ] **11** Ezek 25-27, Ps 38

- [ ] **12** Ezek 28-30, Ps 39
- [ ] **13** Ezek 31-33, Ps 40
- [ ] **14** Ezek 34-36, Ps 41
- [ ] **15** Ezek 37-39, Ps 42
- [ ] **16** Ezek 40-44, Ps 43
- [ ] **17** Ezek 45-48, Ps 44
- [ ] **18** Ezra 1-3, Ps 45
- [ ] **19** Ezra 4-7, Ps 46
- [ ] **20** Ezra 8-10, Ps 47
- [ ] **21** Neh 1-3, Ps 48
- [ ] **22** Neh 4-6, Ps 49

- [ ] **23** Neh 7-9, Ps 50
- [ ] **24** Neh 10-11, Ps 51
- [ ] **25** Neh 12-13, Ps 52
- [ ] **26** Esther 1-5, Ps 53
- [ ] **27** Esther 6-10, Ps 54
- [ ] **28** Dan 1-3, Ps 55
- [ ] **29** Dan 4-6, Ps 56
- [ ] **30** Dan 7-9, Ps 57
- [ ] **31** Dan 10-12, Ps 58

August

- [ ] **1** Hag 1-2, Ps 59
- [ ] **2** Zech 1-4, Ps 60
- [ ] **3** Zech 5-8, Ps 61
- [ ] **4** Zech 9-14, Ps 62
- [ ] **5** Mal 1-2, Ps 63
- [ ] **6** Mal 3-4, Ps 64
- [ ] **7** 1 Chron 1-10, Ps 65
- [ ] **8** 1 Chron 11-14, Ps 66
- [ ] **9** 1 Chron 15-17, Ps 67
- [ ] **10** 1 Chron 18-21, Ps 68
- [ ] **11** 1 Chron 22-24, Ps 69
- [ ] **12** 1 Chron 25-29, Ps 70
- [ ] **13** 2 Chron 1-4, Ps 71
- [ ] **14** 2 Chron 5-8, Ps 72
- [ ] **15** 2 Chron 9-12, Ps 73
- [ ] **16** 2 Chron 13-17, Ps 74
- [ ] **17** 2 Chron 18-20, Ps 75
- [ ] **18** 2 Chron 21-24, Ps 76
- [ ] **19** 2 Chron 25-27, Ps 77
- [ ] **20** 2 Chron 28-31, Ps 78
- [ ] **21** 2 Chron 32-34, Ps 79
- [ ] **22** 2 Chron 35-36, Ps 80
- [ ] **23** Matt 1-2, Ps 81
- [ ] **24** Matt 3-4, Ps 82
- [ ] **25** Matt 5-6, Ps 83
- [ ] **26** Matt 7-8, Ps 84
- [ ] **27** Matt 9-10, Ps 85
- [ ] **28** Matt 11-12, Ps 86
- [ ] **29** Matt 13-14, Ps 87
- [ ] **30** Matt 15-16, Ps 88
- [ ] **31** Matt 17-18, Ps 89

September

- [ ] **1** Matt 19-20, Ps 90
- [ ] **2** Matt 21-22, Ps 91
- [ ] **3** Matt 23-24, Ps 92
- [ ] **4** Matt 25-26, Ps 93
- [ ] **5** Matt 27-28, Ps 94
- [ ] **6** Mark 1-2, Ps 95
- [ ] **7** Mark 3-4, Ps 96
- [ ] **8** Mark 5-6, Ps 97
- [ ] **9** Mark 7-8, Ps 98
- [ ] **10** Mark 9-10, Ps 99
- [ ] **11** Mark 11-12, Ps 100
- [ ] **12** Mark 13-14, Ps 101
- [ ] **13** Mark 15-16, Ps 102
- [ ] **14** John 1-2, Ps 103
- [ ] **15** John 3-4, Ps 104
- [ ] **16** John 5-6, Ps 105
- [ ] **17** John 7-8, Ps 106
- [ ] **18** John 9-10, Ps 107
- [ ] **19** John 11-12, Ps 108
- [ ] **20** John 13-15, Ps 109
- [ ] **21** John 16-18, Ps 110
- [ ] **22** John 19-21, Ps 111
- [ ] **23** Luke 1, Ps 112
- [ ] **24** Luke 2-3, Ps 113
- [ ] **25** Luke 4-5, Ps 114
- [ ] **26** Luke 6-7, Ps 115
- [ ] **27** Luke 8-9, Ps 116
- [ ] **28** Luke 10-11, Ps 117
- [ ] **29** Luke 12-13, Ps 118
- [ ] **30** Luke 14-16, Ps 119:1-32

October

- ☐ **1** Luke 17-18, Ps 119:33-64
- ☐ **2** Luke 19-20, Ps 119:65-96
- ☐ **3** Luke 21-22, Ps 119:97-128
- ☐ **4** Luke 23-24, Ps 119:129-152
- ☐ **5** Acts 1-2, Ps 119:153-176
- ☐ **6** Acts 3-4, Ps 120
- ☐ **7** Acts 5-6, Ps 121
- ☐ **8** Acts 7-8, Ps 122
- ☐ **9** Acts 9-10, Ps 123
- ☐ **10** Acts 11-12, Ps 124
- ☐ **11** Acts 13-14, Ps 125
- ☐ **12** Acts 15-16, Ps 126
- ☐ **13** Acts 17-18, Ps 127
- ☐ **14** Acts 19-20, Ps 128
- ☐ **15** Acts 21-22, Ps 129
- ☐ **16** Acts 23-24, Ps 130
- ☐ **17** Acts 25-26, Ps 131
- ☐ **18** Acts 27-28, Ps 132
- ☐ **19** Rom 1-2, Ps 133
- ☐ **20** Rom 3-4, Ps 134
- ☐ **21** Rom 5-6, Ps 135
- ☐ **22** Rom 7-8, Ps 136
- ☐ **23** Rom 9-10, Ps 137
- ☐ **24** Rom 11-12, Ps 138
- ☐ **25** Rom 13-14, Ps 139
- ☐ **26** Rom 15-16, Ps 140
- ☐ **27** 1 Cor 1-2, Ps 141
- ☐ **28** 1 Cor 3-4, Ps 142
- ☐ **29** 1 Cor 5-6, Ps 143
- ☐ **30** 1 Cor 7-8, Ps 144
- ☐ **31** 1 Cor 9-10, Ps 145

November

- ☐ **1** 1 Cor 11-12, Ps 146
- ☐ **2** 1 Cor 13-14, Ps 147
- ☐ **3** 1 Cor 15-16, Ps 148
- ☐ **4** 2 Cor 1-2, Ps 149
- ☐ **5** 2 Cor 3-4, Ps 150
- ☐ **6** 2 Cor 5-6, Ps 1
- ☐ **7** 2 Cor 7-8, Ps 2
- ☐ **8** 2 Cor 9-10, Ps 3
- ☐ **9** 2 Cor 11-13, Ps 4
- ☐ **10** Gal 1-2, Ps 5
- ☐ **11** Gal 3-4, Ps 6
- ☐ **12** Gal 5-6, Ps 7
- ☐ **13** Eph 1-2, Ps 8
- ☐ **14** Eph 3-4, Ps 9
- ☐ **15** Eph 5-6, Ps 10
- ☐ **16** Phil 1-2, Ps 11
- ☐ **17** Phil 3-4, Ps 12
- ☐ **18** Col 1-2, Ps 13
- ☐ **19** Col 3-4, Ps 14
- ☐ **20** 1 Thess 1-2, Ps 15
- ☐ **21** 1 Thess 3-4, Ps 16
- ☐ **22** 1 Thess 5, Ps 17
- ☐ **23** 2 Thess 1-3, Ps 18
- ☐ **24** 1 Tim 1-2, Ps 19
- ☐ **25** 1 Tim 3-4, Ps 20
- ☐ **26** 1 Tim 5-6, Ps 21
- ☐ **27** 2 Tim 1-4, Ps 22
- ☐ **28** Titus, Ps 23
- ☐ **29** Philem, Ps 24
- ☐ **30** Heb 1-2, Ps 25

December

- [ ] **1** Heb 3-4, Ps 26
- [ ] **2** Heb 5-6, Ps 27
- [ ] **3** Heb 7-8, Ps 28
- [ ] **4** Heb 9-10, Ps 29
- [ ] **5** Heb 11-13, Ps 30
- [ ] **6** James 1-3, Ps 31
- [ ] **7** James 4-5, Ps 32
- [ ] **8** 1 Pet 1-2, Ps 33

- [ ] **9** 1 Pet 3-5, Ps 34
- [ ] **10** 2 Pet 1-3, Ps 35
- [ ] **11** 1 John 1-2, Ps 36
- [ ] **12** 1 John 3-4, Ps 37
- [ ] **13** 1 John 5, 2 John, 3 John, Ps 38
- [ ] **14** Jude, Ps 39
- [ ] **15** Rev 1-3, Ps 40

- [ ] **16** Rev 4-6, Ps 41
- [ ] **17** Rev 7-9, Ps 42
- [ ] **18** Rev 10-11, Ps 43
- [ ] **19** Rev 12-13, Ps 44
- [ ] **20** Rev 14-16, Ps 45
- [ ] **21** Rev 17-18, Ps 46
- [ ] **22** Rev 19-20, Ps 47
- [ ] **23** Rev 21-22, Ps 48

A Day in the Life

DAY 1
SEARCH THE SCRIPTURES—1 CHRONICLES 12

While you can typically find me at my desk surrounded by my study tools, this morning found me in my bed. I was reading about the men who came alongside David. Mighty, legendary men who stood by his side and helped him. The *Search the Scriptures* question prompted a comparison between 1 Chronicles 12 and 1 Corinthians 12:

> *Observe the unity prevailing at this time among the followers of David—though drawn from so many different tribes—and also the diversity of gifts which were found among them. Make a list of these gifts and compare them with the gifts of the Spirit as set forth in 1 Corinthians 12:4-11.1*

I turned to the prompted passage and read a list I knew very well. I had known what my spiritual gifts were in my early twenties, and the thought never occurred to me that they would change. But this time, as I read the familiar section of Scripture, one of the gifts hit me differently. My heart quickened at the word as if seeing it for the first time: *faith*.

I recognized the familiar feeling of an impending trail of cross-references and began the process of digging.

STEP 1: CROSS-REFERENCE

There was one cross-reference provided for that first part of 1 Corinthians 12:9 in my Bible's margin, but it wasn't relevant to my study. So I proceeded through my Scripture study system.

STEP 2: LEXICON

Using the Blue Letter Bible app on my phone, I looked up 1 Corinthians 12:9 and tapped on the verse. Then I tapped on the phrase "Interlinear" and found the Greek word for faith: *pistis*. I tapped the word to open the Lexicon and saw nine different definitions that could be used for the word *faith*. I didn't stay there long. Because *faith* is a common word in the Bible, it would have taken me forever to dig through every single example listed. So I moved along quickly to the next step.

STEP 3: COMMENTARY

While still in the Blue Letter Bible app, I clicked on "Commentaries" and scrolled down to my first go-to: Jamieson, Fausset, and Brown (or as I refer to it, *JFB*). I always go there first because of the simplicity with which the text is displayed. The verses are separated into a numerical list corresponding with the verse number, and the comments are included as the numbered point. If you're studying a particular word or phrase rather than an overall chapter or concept, JFB is one of the best places to start. I tapped on "Commentary on 1 Corinthians 12" and scanned the paragraph of commentary on verses 8-10 until I found that heart-quickening word:

> Gifts dependent on a special *faith*, namely, that of miracles (Matthew 17:20).[2]

I followed the trail to Matthew and read the story in context. Read Matthew 17:14-21, and then write verses 19-20 here:

_____

_____

_____

_____

_____

Because of your unbelief, I wrote in my journal. There was a superscript number next to the word in my Bible representing an alternative translation, so I looked to the margin. *Unbelief is also translated "little faith."* The cross-reference wasn't listed, but I thought of Lazarus and the words Jesus spoke just before He raised him from the dead:

> Jesus said to her, "Did I not say to you that if you would believe you would see the glory of God?" (John 11:40).

The gift of faith as listed in 1 Corinthians 12:9 is the faith of miracles. It is the faith of trusting in the fulfillment of a divine promise. The kind of faith where He provides the building-stones and I piece them together. The kind where He repeats the same three words—*womb, watch, wait*—over and over, day after day, month after month, as markers of His glory-trail. And I knew I was on the path of mercy.

I went in search of a verse in Judges that was referenced in another commentary, and I was confused for a moment by what I was reading. The story didn't match up with the topic of faith. Then I realized I was in the book of Joshua, not Judges. It was part of a pattern of misread references I recognized a couple of years ago as a way that God steers my quiet times to the places He wants me to settle into, camp at, and chew on. So I read until it made sense. Because I knew it would—it always does eventually.

I was in Joshua 4—the story of the memorial stones. Rocks had been picked up from the deepest part of the Jordan River by twelve men representing each of the twelve tribes of Israel. The same tribes that had just walked across the Jordan River on dry ground. This accidental cross-reference had a twofold significance:

1. The men were told to set up the stones they had gathered as a sign, in anticipation of their children asking about them in the future. The stones would prompt them to retell their miracle story.

2. The miracle story that would be retold to future generations included the very same men I was reading about in 1 Chronicles 12. Mighty, legendary men who stood by David's side and helped him.

And it all came full circle. God told Joshua to instruct the men to set up the memorial to provide an occasion for the children to ask their parents what it meant. (With my color-coded system, I noticed that this phrase was repeated in Joshua 4:6 as well as 4:21. I boxed them out in orange and drew a line connecting them.)

The stones were the memorial of the miracle. And the questions of their children in the future kept the memory alive through the retelling of the story. In my mind, those men were setting up a memorial to not only remember the miracle God had just done, but also as an act of faith, believing that He would give them the children and grandchildren (and generations more), to retell their story.

As I wrapped up my quiet time that morning, I finished with looking at a cross-reference from a Sunday morning message that I had written in the margin next to Joshua 4:6, and I smiled as He handed me another stone for my faith-building memorial. One that was being built *before* the miracle instead of after like Joshua's. One that anticipated the miracle.

> This will be written for the generation to come,
> That a people yet to be created may praise the LORD (Psalm 102:18).

SUMMARY OF VERSES

- 1 Chronicles 12
- 1 Corinthians 12:4-11 (specifically the first part of verse 9)
- Joshua 4
- Psalm 102:18

DAY 2

ASKING FOR WISDOM—JAMES 1:5-6

When I sit down for my morning quiet time, *Search the Scriptures* is always within reach. But I don't always use it. (That's why it's taken me more than ten years to get through it.) When I do use it to guide my time studying Scripture, it often triggers a curiosity about a word or topic that I'll spend a couple of days chasing down. The previous day's time spent in 1 Chronicles 12 was no different. I was thinking about the gift of faith a lot, and I needed to dig deeper.

I thought of James. His entire book talks heavily about faith. So I went there first, and it didn't take long before I found a phrase that, once again, caught my attention.

Read James 1:2-8, and then write verses 5-6 here:

_____

_____

_____

_____

_____

STEP 1: CROSS-REFERENCE

There was one cross-reference provided for that first part of James 1:5 in my Bible's margin, given to the phrase "if any of you lacks wisdom." Flip over to 1 Kings 3:9 and write it here:

_____

_____

_____

_____

Now, go back to the beginning of 1 Kings 3 and read verses 1–15 for context. This is when I bring back my old-school SOAP method, observing and summarizing what's happening in the chapter—the details that sort of jump off the page at me:

1. Solomon loved the Lord, but he still made mistakes. It says it right there in black and white in verse 3. He loved God...except he still did things that only priests were allowed to do in places that were not the tabernacle. The key here, though, is that God knew his heart. He knew his intentions were good. And we know that because although Solomon made his own sacrifice at Gibeon, God still spoke to him.

2. Solomon was terrified of his position as king. He was thrown into the deep end of running an entire nation of people and didn't know the first thing about it. He felt young. Naïve. And helpless. And just when he was trying to figure it out as he went, making sacrifices when he could, God recognized that he was trying. And told him to just ask for the thing he lacked but needed so desperately in order to do his job successfully. Just. Ask.

3. Solomon prayed. And it was a prayer God honored. I love when Scripture explains Scripture because it removes any and all guesswork from the equation. In this particular chapter, we see three things: what Solomon prayed, how God answered, and why He answered the way He did.

Re-read verse nine. What did Solomon ask for and why did he ask for it?

_____

_____

_____

_____

_____

There was a superscript number next to the word *understanding* in my Bible, representing an alternate translation, so I looked in the margin. The note read, "Understanding is also translated *hearing*." Therefore, Solomon's prayer (in its purest form) was: *Give me a hearing heart.*

STEP 2: LEXICON

Using the Blue Letter Bible app, I looked up 1 Kings 3:9 and tapped on the verse. Then I tapped on the phrase "Interlinear" and found the Hebrew word for *understanding*. I tapped the word to open the Lexicon and skimmed the text until I found the reference for 1 Kings 3:9. I had my clear definition, along with even more cross-references (including Genesis 11:7 and 42:23).

A cursory read of these verses shows that they both refer to understanding foreign languages. Hearing when others assume you don't know what they are talking about. Having the ability to hear and translate and understand what is being spoken. Solomon was desperate to hear God and not be confused by what he heard. He didn't have time for it to get lost in translation through someone else's interpretation. He needed to lead God's people well. And he needed God Himself to instruct him in order to do his job effectively. So he asked for an understanding, hearing heart. One that discerns between good and evil. One that does not lack wisdom.

Re-read verses 11-14. How did God answer Solomon's prayer? What did He give him?

_____

_____

_____

_____

_____

The Amplified version of the verse that started the cross-reference trail reads this way:

> If any of you lacks wisdom [to guide him through a decision or circumstance], he is to ask of [our benevolent] God, who gives to everyone generously and without rebuke or blame, and it will be given to him (James 1:5 AMP).

God heard Solomon's prayer. Even when he asked after offering profane and unholy sacrifices that were not according to the very specific and strict instructions God gave to Moses in Leviticus, He still heard. And He gave generously, without rebuke or blame or scolding. Because isn't that how His mercy works?

Thank You, Lord, for the way You love us.

DAY 3
STITCHING AND CRAVING—JAMES 1:5-6

Since I barely got into the two verses of James before jumping ship and following the cross-reference to 1 Kings on day 2, I began my day by picking up where I left off. Re-read James 1:5-6 and write the verses here:

_____

_____

_____

_____

Once again, we hit the ground running with a cross-reference. This time, it's for the phrase "let him ask of God," and it's pointing to Matthew 7:7. Read it, then write it here:

_____

_____

_____

STEP 1: CROSS-REFERENCE

Because I can't ignore the cross-reference symbol, I chased down the one that was assigned to this verse in Matthew, which led me to four more verses after that, and then two more still after. Since you're walking with me step-by-step, look up these verses:

- Mark 11:24
- Luke 11:9 AMPC
- Jeremiah 33:3

- 1 John 3:22 and 5:14-15
- John 14:13

When I read cross-references, I don't read them as separate entities. I read them as if more than one person is telling a story at the same time, and each one pipes in with a new detail that the other didn't include. I stitch them together to tell the complete story. And when I did that with these verses (combined with James 1:5), I got a much richer version of the lesson.

> If any of you lacks wisdom that will guide you through a decision or circumstance, ask Me and it will be given to you. Whatever things you ask, believe that you receive them, and you will have them. So I'll say it again: ask, and keep asking! Seek, and keep seeking! Knock, and keep knocking! Because when you call to Me, I will answer you and show you great and mighty and inaccessible things which you do not know. And I will give it to you because you keep My commandments and do what is pleasing in My sight. When you ask anything according to My will, I hear you. And because you know I hear, you also know that you will have the petitions that you have asked me for. Because whatever you ask in My name, I will do it, that I may be glorified.

That's about the time that I write "Wow!" in my prayer journal—in moments like that, when He shows up and stitches together the fabric of truth that is hidden behind one simple five-word phrase. When He does what He says He will do in Jeremiah 33:3, telling us "great and hidden things" (ESV). When He makes the hidden parts of His Word accessible simply because we are curious. He honors our curious-wonder, and in it, He glorifies Himself. I love it when He does that.

STEP 2: LEXICON

Using the Blue Letter Bible app, I looked up James 1:5 and found the Greek word for "let him ask." When I parsed the verb, I noticed that it's in the imperative mood, which is not at all an invitation. It's an absolute command requiring full obedience on the part of all hearers.

Okay. This is a big deal. Now I need to look deeper at the definition of what it is I am being commanded to do. Because in order to fully obey, I need to understand. (Lord, give me an understanding heart!) I tapped on the Greek word *aiteo*. It means "to beg, crave, desire."

Now I know how to ask. Rather than praying, "God, give me the kind of wisdom that comes with an understanding and hearing heart," I can confidently pray, "God, help me to crave the kind of wisdom that comes with an understanding and hearing heart."

Interestingly enough, *aiteo* is only translated as "crave" once, and it's only rendered that way in the King James Version. It's in Mark 15 when Joseph of Arimathea (a prominent and well-respected member of the Jewish high court) went before Pilate after Jesus died (and was still hanging on the cross) and asked for His body so he could bury Him. The King James Version translates it this way:

> Joseph of Arimathaea, an honourable counsellor, which also waited for the kingdom of God, came, and went in boldly unto Pilate, and craved the body of Jesus (Mark 15:43).

STEP 3: COMMENTARY

When I looked up Matthew Henry's commentary on Mark 15:43, I saw the story through another set of eyes and heard it from another understanding heart.

> *Joseph went in boldly to Pilate*; though he knew how much it would affront the chief priests, who had loaded him with so much reproach, to see any honour done him, yet *he put on courage*; perhaps at first he was a little afraid, but *taking heart on it*, he determined to show this respect to the remains of the Lord Jesus, let the worst come to the worst.[3]

Joseph came out of the woodwork. He was a "secret" disciple—believing in Jesus as the Messiah, though he likely did not openly profess it. Until he stood before his boss and boldly asked for the body of the Man he had just killed.

Matthew Henry also comments on the parallel story in Matthew 27, noting that Joseph stepped up when the story was still bleak. Before the resurrection, when the outcome didn't make sense and all the apostles had fled, Joseph couldn't just let it be. Before the miracle, Joseph asked in faith. So he could prepare for the miracle that he couldn't possibly know was about to happen.

Joseph *craved* Jesus—even in His death. When the glory was still unseen, he craved Him.

If anyone lacks wisdom, let us crave Him. *Oh Lord, let me crave You.*

DAY 4
A WOVEN HOPE—JAMES 1:5-6

Let's pick it up again right where we left off last time. Re-read James 1:5-6, and then write the verses here:

As usual, we will start right away with chasing down a cross-reference. This morning, it's for the phrase "it will be given to him," and it's pointing to Jeremiah 29:12. Read it, then write it here:

For context, back and up and read Jeremiah 29:10-14. When you do, you will come across one of the most famous verses outside of John 3:16. I want to dig into that verse a little deeper this morning, to make sure we're understanding it correctly and to see how it explains this passage in James a little more clearly.

STEP 1: CROSS-REFERENCE

In order to understand Jeremiah 29:12, we need to know what verse 11 is saying. There wasn't a cross-reference listed for the verse in my Bible, so I skipped ahead to the next step in my study-Scripture system.

STEP 2: LEXICON

Using the Blue Letter Bible app, I look up Jeremiah 29:11 and find the Hebrew word for "the thoughts." *Plan. Purpose. Invention.* I went back to the list of words in the verse, this time tapping on the "parse" button for the phrase "that I think," and I saw that the stem is qal. I closed the pop-up and tapped on the Hebrew word, *chashab*, paying close attention to the qal distinction. Inside the Gesenius lexicon, I saw an interesting phrase: "a weaver mixing threads and colors."

The illustration came alive for me. As God thinks about me, He simultaneously weaves threads and colors that create the tapestry of my life story.

And then things got even more interesting. This is how the King James Version translates Jeremiah 29:11:

> "I know the thoughts that I think toward you," saith the LORD, "thoughts
> of peace, and not of evil, to give you an expected end."

The Hebrew definition for that phrase "you an expected," as discovered in the lexicon, first means "cord." Then it lists additional definitions: hope, ground for hope, things hoped for, expectation, outcome. It struck a chord in me. Also translated *rope*, the first cross-reference given was Joshua 2:18, 21. It's the familiar story of Rahab, a prostitute, hiding two men that Joshua sends in to spy out the land. The king had caught wind of their plan and was looking to flush them out. Rahab knew that God had given the Israelites the land of Jericho, and it was only a matter of time before life as she knew it would end. She knew her entire family would be killed. And in exchange for hiding them, she asked the two men to spare her and her family.

They agreed. And they told her to bring her family into her home and to hang a line of scarlet cord in her window. When they came back to take the city, they would see the cord in the window and spare them.

So she did as she was told and hung the cord. And she waited, in faith, that their lives would be spared. The very next chapter is the parting of the Red Sea, followed by the memorial stones that we started with on Day 1. It's not until chapter six that her faith was rewarded. All that time, she waited. Looking at the daily reminder that hung in her window...until the day Jericho was destroyed. And she and her family were spared.

There's an important lesson here on the timing of answered prayer: It doesn't always come right away. God tells us very specifically in James 1:5 that when we ask, it will be given to us. But He doesn't say when. It could be immediate. It could be days or weeks. Or it could be years later. But the conversation is ongoing. If we piece together everything we've learned so far, we can add on to our stitched-together Scripture from yesterday:

> If any of you lacks wisdom that will guide you through a decision or circumstance, ask Me and it will be given to you. Whatever things you ask, believe that you receive them, and you will have them. So I'll say it again: ask, and keep asking! Seek, and keep seeking! Knock, and keep knocking! Because when you call to Me, I will answer you and show you great and mighty and inaccessible things which you do not know. And I will give it to you because you keep My commandments and do what is pleasing in My sight. When you ask anything according to My will, I hear you. And because you know I hear, you also know that you will have the petitions that you have asked me for. Because whatever you ask in My name, I will do it, that I may be glorified. And until I do, while I am mixing the threads

and colors and pulling everything together, here's a little piece. A little snippet of what's to come as part of a divine promise. Take it. Hang it up. Look at it. And remember: I will do this. Then you will call upon me and pray to Me. And while I'm weaving, I will listen to you.

STEP 3: COMMENTARY

Go back to James 1 and find the commentaries for it on the Blue Letter Bible app. I love how JFB expounds upon the phrase "upbraideth not" or "without reproach."

> [It is] an illustration of God's giving *simply*. He gives to the humble suppliant without upbraiding him with his past sin and ingratitude, or his future abuse of God's goodness. The Jews pray, "Let me not have need of the gifts of men, whose gifts are few, but their upbraidings manifold; but give me out of Thy large and full hand." Compare Solomon's prayer for "wisdom," and God's gift above what he asked, though God foresaw his future abuse of His goodness would deserve very differently.[4]

God looked past Solomon's presumptuous sacrifices. And He didn't stop to scold Rahab about her lifestyle before sparing her life. He gave simply. He listened fully. Oh, the glorious and undeserved grace—that He still hears our prayers.

DAY 5

MOVING MOUNTAINS—JAMES 1:5-6

Welcome back! You're five days in and still coming back for more. I love that you're discovering hidden truths in God's Word with me, step-by-step. I pray that these tools will provide the resources for you to create your own study-Scripture system—one that paves the way for God to speak in a way that is unique to you, in a voice you recognize daily.

I'm not quite finished with picking apart our New Testament verses, so re-read James 1:5-6, then write the verses here:

_____

_____

_____

_____

_____

STEP 1: CROSS-REFERENCE

In my Bible, there is a symbol by the phrase "but let him ask in faith, with no doubting," indicating a cross-reference. It points to Mark 11:23-24. Read the verses, then write them here:

_____

_____

_____

_____

_____

If you aren't already familiar with the Gospels, the books of Matthew, Mark, and Luke all contain similar stories that are often written with a similar sequence and wording. John was likely written later than the other three Gospels and is not as heavily influenced by them. Because of that, there are a couple of additional cross-references to this same story in Matthew, but the one in Luke is the one that I pay attention to. It's essentially the same. But instead of moving a mountain into the sea, it's a mulberry tree:

The apostles said to the Lord, "Increase our faith." So the Lord said, "If you have faith as a mustard seed, you can say to this mulberry tree, 'Be pulled up by the roots and be planted in the sea,' and it would obey you" (Luke 17:5-6).

Keep your finger in Luke and hop over to another, seemingly unrelated story in 1 Chronicles 14. There's a story between verses 8 and 17 about David defeating the Philistines. In verse 15, God tells him to wait to do anything until he hears one particular thing. What is it?

David had the Philistines in his sights. He'd already defeated them once just a few verses before, and he knew God was on his side. He very easily could have just gone on with both barrels blazing.

But he stopped. And checked in with God one more time. And God said, "I'm going to do things a little differently this time. This time, you're not going to go after them."

In fact, He told David to turn his men entirely away from them and steal away over to the grove of mulberry trees and wait. While they waited, they were to listen for the sound of marching at the top of the trees. Only then were they to move.

I can imagine what David's soldiers would have said. "You're crazy! That is absolutely insane! *They are right there*. And we're going to hide behind some trees and wait for a noise?"

Oh, the faith it must have taken for David to make the backward, game-time decision to not do anything. To stand there huddled in the grove, waiting for a marching sound in the tops of the trees that would signal the green light to go and to go now.

Flip back over to Luke 17 and re-read verse 5. What did the apostles want God to do?

And how did God reply in verse 6?

Now, look how the Amplified Bible interprets verses 5 and 6:

The apostles said to the Lord, "Increase our faith [our ability to confidently trust in God and in His power]." And the Lord said, "If you have [confident, abiding] faith in God [even as small] as a mustard seed, you could say to this mulberry tree [which has very strong roots], 'Be pulled up by the roots and be planted in the sea'; and [if the request was in agreement with the will of God] it would have obeyed you" (Luke 17:5-6 AMP).

There is a footnote there in the Amplified Bible after the verse, saying that "Jesus used this moment to emphasize that a person's confident, abiding faith combined with God's will and power can produce absolutely amazing results. God is fully capable of doing that which man regards as impossible."[5]

Those words are inspiring, empowering, and encouraging all on their own. But when you combine them with the 1 Chronicles 14 story of David and his army at the grove of mulberry trees, they take on an entirely new meaning.

Without any context, I would imagine David with an army of maybe 20 men in a small grove of trees. But if you do the math of David's army from 1 Chronicles 12, he actually has an army of 300,000 men. That's a population roughly the size of Pittsburgh!

Nothing in the text between 1 Chronicles 13 and the moment before this battle in chapter 14 indicates any loss of men (aside from Uzza in chapter 13), and nothing indicates a smaller group of men were taken for this particular battle. So it's safe to assume that the entire population-of-Pittsburgh army was there.

God told them to circle around the Philistines to come upon them in a surprise attack in front of those mulberry trees. And this is how the scene plays out in my mind: David is leading a gigantic army. God tells him to go to the mulberry trees and listen for the sound of marching in the tops of the trees. So he has to be close enough to the trees to hear the noise. In my mind, David is in front of the trees with the captains of his army, and the rest of the men are behind them. He waits. And listens. And hears the sound of the marching and moves forward in faith and pushes the enemy back at least 18 miles.

When you have the faith to look at a mulberry tree and tell it to be pulled up by the roots and be planted in the sea, you are believing in faith that God will remove any obstacle between you and the thing He has called you to. The thing you are believing Him for. The thing that you are believing His divine power to do.

It's the faith of miracles.

He will pull up that mulberry tree by the root so that as you move forward confidently, you will not trip on any lingering obstacle. And the moment you step out, after He has directed you to do so, the enemy will be driven back so far that you cannot see him with your naked eye. And you can walk forward confidently in the direction of the destiny He has planned for you, victoriously following His footsteps. For His glory.

That's the kind of faith He calls us to.

But before we leave this story in 1 Chronicles 14, there's one more thing you need to see. Go to Blue Letter Bible and look up the phrase *of the mulberry trees* in verse 15. According-ing to the Outline of Biblical Usage, what is the second definition of the Hebrew word?

That Psalm 84:6 reference? It's our *dig your well* trail marker.

Now that we've chased down the cross-references, I want to drop by Mark one more time and do a little more digging.

STEP 2: LEXICON

Using the Blue Letter Bible app on my phone, I look up Mark 11:23, tap on "Interlinear," and find the Greek word for *mountain.* Toward the end of the lexicon definition, I find the rich treasure I'm looking for:

> to remove mountains, *i.e. to accomplish most difficult, stupendous, incredible things*[6]

STEP 3: COMMENTARY

I look through the commentaries and am struck by Matthew Henry's insights:

> The removing of mountains…may be applied to that *miracle of faith*, which all true Christians are endued with. *It justifies* us (Rom. 5:1), and so removes the mountains of guilt, and casts them into the *depths of the sea*, never to rise up in judgment against us, Mic. 7:19. It *purifies* the heart (Acts 15:9), and so removes mountains of corruption, and *makes them plains* before the grace of God, Zec. 4:7.[7]

DAY 6
WITH NO DOUBTING—JAMES 1:5-6

As I was studying for today's homework in James 1:6, I must confess: It started a little slow. There were no cross-references in my Bible for the description James gives for doubting, so I moved on to the lexicon. I clicked on a couple of different words and began chasing down the cross-references included. I was beginning to think that this was going to be one of those mornings that don't really lead to a mind-blowing connection—when I could simply read His Word and thank Him for His presence. Because they do happen, and that's okay.

I chased down a dozen different cross-references, flipping back and forth between the Old Testament and the New before ending up in Psalm 107. All of the references were fantastic examples of things I could accurately use to teach on James 1:6. But Psalm 107? It was twelve degrees of separation from James. But it's where God clearly and specifically had me for the purpose of this study. You'll see why in a minute.

We're going to jump into the middle of the psalm this morning. Read Psalm 107:23-32.

The psalmist is speaking of the men who do business on the ships in the ocean. He describes how they see the works of the Lord on the face of the sea. They recognize His wonders in the deep. They knew that they were entirely powerless against the power of the ocean. The strength of storms and when they would pick up...God commanded it all. The raising up of the stormy wind and also the calming of the waves. I think you can probably see how this ties back to James 1:6, but stick with me a little bit further. This is where it gets interesting.

Verse 27 describes the seafarers in the midst of a storm, reeling to and fro and staggering like drunken men. They were unable to walk straight because of the way the ship was violently being tossed back and forth. And their fear in such a scenario left them at their wits' end.

There is a note in the margin of my Bible in front of the phrase "are at their wits' end," indicating an alternative translation. One that is different in meaning from the words in the text but is justified by the original languages. In other words, the translators could have understood the original word or phrase in this other way: *All their wisdom is swallowed up.*

I went to the lexicon to see it for myself. The Hebrew phrase is *chokmah bala'*. When combined with the proper parsing, the definition literally reads: "wisdom to be ended."

When the men are at this point—at their wits' end—they cry out to the Lord. What happens when they do that in Psalm 107:29-30?

_____

_____

_____

Let's combine everything we've learned in James 1:5-6 with this new information we've learned from Psalm 107, adding to the narrative we've already built over the last couple of days:

> If any of you lacks wisdom, ask Me and it will be given to you. Whatever things you ask, believe that you receive them, and you will have them. So I'll say it again: ask, and keep asking! Seek, and keep seeking! Knock, and keep knocking! Because when you call to Me, I will answer you and show you great and mighty and inaccessible things which you do not know. And I will give it to you because you keep My commandments and do what is pleasing in My sight. When you ask anything according to My will, I hear you. And because you know I hear, you also know that you will have the petitions that you have asked me for. Because whatever you ask in My name, I will do it, that I may be glorified. And until I do, while I am mixing the threads and colors and pulling everything together, here's a little piece. A little snippet of what's to come as part of a divine promise. Take it. Hang it up. Look at it. And remember: I will do this. Then you will call upon Me and pray to Me. And while I'm weaving, I will listen to you.

> While I'm working and weaving, and while you wait, you will probably start to overthink. You will begin wavering on what you think I told you, second-guessing that little string in your hand. Staggering like a drunken man while your doubts make you reel to and fro as if you're on a ship on a stormy sea. And that wisdom you asked Me for? You'll feel like you've lost it. Like it's been swallowed up by the very sea that's creating the instability in your mind. Then you'll be back to the point of needing wisdom

refreshed. So ask Me again. Keep asking! I'll calm the storm. And still the waves. And strengthen your faith as I repeat My promise to you. And eventually, when My time is right, you will be glad. Because the waves will be quiet, and I will guide you to your desired haven.

It's imperative to remember that we need to ask God, and then *keep asking.* Asking in faith and believing in faith that He gives to all liberally and without reproach, being extremely careful to remove any doubt. And the best way to remove the doubt that tosses us like a wave which is, itself, tossed by the wind? Asking God to calm the storm. The same way He did in Psalm 107. And Matthew 14:22-33. And Mark 4:35-41. And Psalm 89:9. And Psalm 65:7.

Because when He tells us to ask in faith without doubting, He is telling us to ask in faith and allow Him to take care of the doubt.

> Oh that men would give thanks to the LORD for His goodness, and for His wonderful works to the children of men (Psalm 107:8).

DAY 7
A STRENGTHENING FAITH—JAMES 1:5-6

Whew! You've made it all seven days! I hope you discovered new things and learned new ways to study, making God's Word come more alive to you than ever before.

I want to end our time together at one of my personal trail markers—with Abraham and Sarah.

Since we're still in James 1:6, and there aren't any cross-references listed in my Bible, I'm jumping to the second step again: the lexicon. I look up James 1:6, tap on "Interlinear," and find the Greek word for *wavereth.* At the very end of the definition, I find the reference to James and the phrase "nothing doubting, i.e. wholly free from doubt." Then, just a few lines later, I see the phrase "He did not hesitate through lack of faith."

That last definition includes a cross-reference that leads us to Romans 4 and the reminder of a promise that was granted through faith. Specifically, God's promise to Abraham: that through him, all the families of the earth should be blessed.

Abraham had every reason to doubt. He was old—a century old, in fact. And his wife had decades of barrenness and infertility under her belt. In the eyes of doctors and bystanders who knew their history, there was absolutely no grounds for hope. But still, he believed in hope. Read Romans 4:19-21 and write it here:

_____

_____

_____

_____

_____

And here we are with one last example of God forgiving sin—just like He did with Solomon and Rahab. If you know Abraham and Sarah's story, you know that they didn't hold fast to their faith entirely. Sarah gave her maid to her husband to hurry the promise of their family along. But God saw that after all that, they recognized their mistake, and repented, and believed the promise He had spoken to them. And when they did that, a funny thing happened: They became *empowered* by their faith. Strengthened by it.

Two things resulted: First, Abraham believed and it was accounted to him for righteousness. Second, Sarah believed and she received strength to conceive—to receive the promise.

When we ask in faith without doubting, our faith not only empowers us against doubt, it actually ushers in the miracle. Remember looking at the gift of faith at the beginning of this week? The faith of miracles? Abraham did not hesitate through want of faith. He didn't consider the circumstances. He did not doubt or waver in unbelief concerning God's promise because his faith strengthened and empowered him.

Abraham and Sarah are a trail marker to me because God has worn the path back to their story more times than I can count—through cross-references, commentaries, conversations with friends, or even social media posts as I scroll through my feed. Over and over and over again, He whispers His promise to me anew. And the more I write it down and box it out in my journal, the more I believe He's repeating it for a reason. He's promoting my faith in a way that makes it difficult to waver in unbelief concerning it—even after a decade of infertility.

And eventually, when He's done mixing colors and weaving threads, He will give the strength to conceive. Until then, I'll hang my scarlet-cord promise in my window and wait in expectation.

LORD, thank You so much for this time. Thank You for everything You've uncovered this week. Thank you for the complexity and completeness of Your Word. Thank You for peeling back onion layers, for promoting faith, for showing us how to ask for wisdom and how to ask in faith without doubting, knowing that You calm the waves that toss us. More importantly, thank You for setting the table for us, for preparing the feast. I pray that every single person reading this will have a newfound hunger for more of Your Word. Thank You for Your grace and mercy. Amen.

Verse by Verse

DAY 1

PSALM 1:1a

The book of Psalms is the largest book in the Bible, and it also happens to be one of my very favorites. This week we will dig into the first psalm using my study-Scripture method, similar to the last sample study.

As you saw previously, a lot of verse-by-verse study is doing the daily due diligence of digging and gathering information so that you can get the bigger picture at the end. Think of it as getting a new piece to the jigsaw puzzle every morning. You pay attention to the nuances of it—the way this part curves in or that part juts out. You'll explore and dig and take note of particular details that will help you to recognize the subtle patterns found in a single, repeated word later in the week. And by the time the week is over, you'll have a fully formed (and fully assembled) picture.

We will take seven days to explore the six verses of Psalm 1 through word definitions, cross-referencing, and good old-fashioned observation. But first, let's read the psalm in its entirety. Please read Psalm 1.

Go to www.biblegateway.com and look up the Amplified Bible, Classic Edition (AMPC) translation for Psalm 1:1. How does it describe the word *blessed?*

You're going to see this week just how important roots are. We'll start by using Blue

Letter Bible to look at the root-word definition for *blessed*. Go to the website, search for Psalm 1:1, and click on the Strong's link (H835) for the word.

In the Root Word (Etymology) section, click the link (H833) to look at the root of *blessed*. What are a few of the phrases that catch your eye?

Now that we have a little bit of a *blessed* foundation, look back at Psalm 1 in your Bible. According to verse one, what three things does the happy, fortunate, prosperous, and enviable man *not* do?

1. _____

2. _____

3. _____

Let's focus on that first non-action for a minute—not walking in ungodly counsel. Go to Blue Letter Bible to look more closely at the Hebrew word for the phrase "that walketh." First, take note of the parsing. Which stem will you be looking for in the definition?

_____

Go into the Strong's tool, scroll down to the Gesenius' Hebrew-Chaldee Lexicon, and click the link to read the full entry. You'll see five different definitions for the qal stem of the word. This is an example of when you would skim through the definition and look for a reference to Psalm 1:1 (hint: you'll find it in definition #2). What description immediately follows the reference?

_____

_____

_____

It's fairly straightforward, and nothing is really mind-blowing in terms of incredible insight. But look a little bit further and take note of the surrounding descriptions.

In the second definition that is given for the qal stem, what description immediately follows the reference to Mic. 2:11?

_____

What is the very first description that's given in the third definition?

_____

_____

_____

Based on the digging you just did, write a brief synopsis of the first part of Psalm 1:1.

_____

_____

_____

Now think about it all in modern-day language. In what ways can you avoid living according to the counsel of the ungodly? What is the biggest challenge you have in avoiding it? Finish your morning in your prayer journal, turning it all into a specific, Psalm 1:1 application prayer.

DAY 2

PSALM 1:1b

Begin by reading all of Psalm 1 again (you will be repeating this step every day this week). Now re-read verse one and let the words soak in.

If your Bible includes cross-references for verse one, chase them down to see what

Scripture has to say about itself regarding the blessed man who doesn't walk, stand, or sit, with the ungodly, the sinners, and the scornful. My Bible pointed me over to Proverbs 4:14, where Solomon gives a clear (and imperative) two-fold warning. What is it?

The next verse in Proverbs continues the warning: "Avoid it, do not travel on it; turn away from it and pass on" (4:15). A warning doesn't get much stronger than that! Not only are you not to walk on the path of the wicked, you are not to so much as *set foot* on that road. Do you remember what the root word for *blessed* was from yesterday's study? What was it?

Skip the scenic day-trip detour. Avoid the tempting shortcut. Continue straight on your way to blessedness!

I kept following the cross-references in my Bible: Proverbs 4:14 led me to Proverbs 1:15, which led me to Psalm 119:101. And suddenly I had the *why* behind the *do not*.

Read Psalm 119:101. Why is it so important to watch your step and make sure to restrain your feet from every evil way?

The Amplified version takes the *why* behind the restraint one step further: that I may not just *keep* His Word, but that I may *hear, receive, love,* and *obey* it.

Go back to Psalm 1:1, and take a minute to dig into the second action in the "must avoid" list on Blue Letter Bible—you're going to find something interesting. What word is used in the KJV instead of the word *path* in the phrase "stands in the path"?

Click on the Strong's link for the phrase "of sinners" (H2400) and look at the Root Word (Etymology) section. Note the word *intensively* immediately before the root word link.

Now, click on the root word link (H2398). According to the Outline of Biblical Usage, what is the first definition for the root word *chata'*?

The sinners that Psalm 1:1 talks about didn't just kind of miss the way or miss their target by an inch. They intensively, thoroughly, and vigorously missed it. They missed it so dramatically that they weren't even anywhere *close* to it!

Now, put it all together: Blessed is the man who stands not in the _____ of sinners who _____. Because standing in the way of sinners who (at the deepest root of them) dramatically miss the way is the very thing that stands in the way of your relationship with God and hearing, receiving, loving, and obeying His Word.

Let's take one last look at Psalm 1:1 and the seat of the scornful that the blessed man avoids. The original Hebrew describes a person who is deriding someone else—mocking them and scoffing at them the same way the soldiers did to Jesus on the day He was crucified.

Do you want to see the process played out by someone who never thought it would happen to him? Take a look at Peter's story at the end of Luke 22. He walked behind Jesus, following at a distance. John 18 gives a similar account of the story, describing how Peter then stood still and warmed himself by the fire with the people who were mocking Jesus. And then, back in Luke 22, Peter sat down among them.

By the end of Luke 22:61, after the walking and the standing and the sitting, what had Peter done three times?

Situations like this can sneak up on you if you aren't careful, and they can happen to anyone. Even someone like Peter. So it's wise to heed Paul's warning from Romans 12:3:

"Do not think of yourself more highly than you ought to." Don't think that it won't happen to you. That, somewhere along the way, you won't get tripped up. "Think soberly," he says, with a moderate estimation of yourself. Doing everything you can to restrain your feet from wandering off. Keep going, straight ahead, following *closely* behind Jesus, keeping His Word. Hearing it. Receiving it. Loving it. And obeying it.

DAY 3

PSALM 1:2

We spent the last two days digging into the blessed man and the things that he does not do. The counsel he does not heed. The roads he avoids (no matter how great the view). And the seats he refuses to take (no matter how tired he is).

Today, we're going to take a look at what he's busy doing instead of all those other things we just finished digging into. Read Psalm 1 once again, in its entirety, then write verse 2 here:

_____

_____

_____

The majority of our time today will be spent cross-referencing to allow Scripture to provide the allegory to our blessed-is-the-man story, starting with another visit to Psalm 119 and the resolve to restrain your feet that you may keep, hear, receive, love, and obey God's Word. But this time, we're going to back up a ways toward the beginning of Psalm 119. Read verses 9-16.

Did you notice a repeated word right off the bat in verse 9? These eight verses are the means to the end of not standing in the way of sinners. *And it starts by cleansing.* Take a quick peek over at 1 John 1:9—"If we confess our sins, He is faithful and just to forgive us our sins and to *cleanse us* from all unrighteousness." That's where everything starts.

Go back to Psalm 119:9 and look up the word *cleanse* on Blue Letter Bible, making sure to take note of the parsing. According to the Outline of Biblical Usage, what is the definition for that specific stem of the Hebrew word?

It's up to God to make you clean. It's up to you to make every effort to *keep yourself clean*. And the best way to do that is to do what both Psalm 1:2 and Psalm 119:16 describe. What is it?

A quiet time isn't just about gathering book knowledge and intellectual information. It's also about falling more in love with God's Word and, in turn, falling more in love with God. The first of the psalmist's two-part vow in Psalm 119:16 to protect himself from the blessing-stealing pitfalls of Psalm 1:1 is to delight himself in God's statutes. And the word he uses for *delight* paints an incredibly vivid picture.

Go to Blue Letter Bible and read the full entry in the Gesenius' Hebrew-Chaldee Lexicon for the phrase "I will delight." (Hint: don't forget about the parsing!) What is the description that is given for the appropriate stem?

Isn't that what the pursuit of God is all about? To not only follow Him, but to follow *hard* after Him. Up close and personal. Digging in deep and delighting yourself in His Word. Because you will be amazed at the sight of the things that will happen!

Joshua knew all about that. In fact, God picked up where the psalmist left off in a two-part instruction of His own to Joshua after Moses died. Just as he was about to lead the people into their long-awaited and repeatedly promised land. The first thing God instructed Joshua to do in Joshua 1 was to be strong and of good courage (something

He repeated three times in four verses). What is the second piece of instruction that's given in verse 8?

Now we circle back to where we started today, because the meditation instruction that God gave Joshua is the same word that's used in Psalm 1:2. If you dig into the Hebrew word, you'll see an interesting description that's tucked into the middle of the third definition. Meditating on something means to talk to yourself, murmuring in a low voice under your breath. It also means to read something syllable by syllable. Verse by verse. Just like what you are doing right here, right now.

Charles Spurgeon described this process as "read[ing] it by day and think[ing] upon it by night."[1] It's letting the words sit and percolate and soak in, day and night. It's delighting in it. Then standing in amazement at the things that will happen—just like Joshua did, two chapters after God's "be strong and meditate" command, when he crossed over the Jordan River on dry ground.

May we be a people whose delight is in the law of the LORD, both day *and* night.

DAY 4

PSALM 1:3a

Today, everything comes full circle. Everything that we've dug into and investigated and deep-vein mined together from the very beginning of this book is about to pull together in a complete, well-rounded picture. Let it all serve as a reminder to keep on digging, even when your brain is tired and feels a little bit numb and you might even be coasting on autopilot. *Keep digging.* God will reveal Himself in the most unexpected ways. Not only in those miracle moments that take your breath away, but also throughout the course of your regular quiet times. Here and there, sprinkled throughout your days, you'll dig up something that will amaze you.

Open your Bible and read the entirety of Psalm 1 again. (By now, you should be getting very familiar with the words and will likely have parts of it memorized!) We're going to dig into the first part of verse three today. The part that talks about the person who delights in the law of the Lord and meditates on it day and night. According to the very first part of verse three, what will that person be like?

There's a note in the margin of my Bible for the word *rivers* that indicates an alternative translation—different in meaning from the words in the text but justified by the original languages. It notes that *rivers* can also be translated *channels*.

Keep that in mind while you cross-reference over to Jeremiah 17:8 to read a continued description of the person who is planted by the river channels, with roots shot out, spread out, and stretched out strong.

Go to Blue Letter Bible and look up the Hebrew word that's used for the phrase "her roots." What is the last definition of the word that's given in the Outline of Biblical Usage section?

If you look at the full entry for the word in Gesenius' Hebrew-Chaldee Lexicon, you'll see a couple of familiar references: "Figuratively, it is the lowest parts of a thing...of a mountain, Job 28:9; of the sea, Job 36:30."[2]

Wait...Job 28? The deepest part of the sea? When I saw those words, the fireworks started going off in my brain! But God was just getting started with His show. Go to

Job 28 and read verses 1-11, re-familiarizing yourself with the first part that we studied together in our previous chapters. Then write verses 9-10 here:

_____

_____

_____

_____

_____

Did you notice the word you took note of a couple of minutes ago? "He cuts out *channels* in the rocks." But there's one more detail you need to pull out from this section. It's about the rock that is having the channels cut into it. According to verse nine, what kind of rock does the man put his hand on?

_____

Keeping your place in Psalm 1:3 and Jeremiah 17:8, hop over to Exodus 17:1-6 to get an idea as to why the flinty rock is such an important detail in our story. For the sake of time, I'll give away the tucked-away detail about that Exodus 17 rock: It's the same word that's used for *flint* in Job 28. What happened in Exodus 17:6 after Moses struck the flint rock?

_____

_____

_____

This is where the rubber meets the road. Because those deep-vein mines that you've dug out and the rock channels you've carved out? It's all been flint rock—the kind that God made that miracle wilderness-water come out of. The kind that Paul says is Christ Himself. And when those dug-out mountain channels fill with the water of His Spirit, they suddenly become river channels. The ones that you are planted by (Psalm 1:3). The ones that your roots shoot-out, spread out, and stretch out strong into (Jeremiah 17:8).

Friends, your roots are only as strong as the depth to which you dig.

So keep on digging. Day by day. Verse by verse. Syllable by syllable. Carving out the flint rock and mining out the gold so that God can turn those mountain channels into the very rivers that soak your spread-out roots...and plant you firmly in Him.

DAY 5
PSALM 1:3b

Word recognition is key to identifying patterns in Scripture. It's why writing things down is so important during the course of your study—it helps to commit things to memory and provides a written record that you can go back and reference when something sounds familiar.

The patterns can be big, lightbulb moments (like we discovered yesterday) or smaller, tying-it-all-together details that we will look at today.

We're going to revisit Jeremiah 17:8 again today and finish looking at what it has to say about the tree that is planted by the dug-out mountain veins that become river waters. Read it, then put your finger there and flip back over to Job 28:9-10. We already know that the miner puts his hand on the flint rock and cuts out the river channels. What happens after that, at the end of verse 10?

Now, go back to Jeremiah 17:8 and look at the KJV on Blue Letter Bible. When the heat comes, most translations read that the tree with spread-out river roots "will not fear." What does the KJV say?

Not only does the English render the same word, the verses in Jeremiah and Job use the same Hebrew word! And when you see the two statements side by side, it makes sense that the person who delights in the Lord and is planted in His Word with those spread-out roots wouldn't see when heat comes. They're too busy seeing (and being amazed by the sight of) every single precious thing they deep-vein mined in their quiet time!

Now read through to the end of Jeremiah 17:8—about the leaves that will stay green from roots pressed down deep in the constant water source. This water source is perpetually supplied from continual digging and is so predictable that when a physical drought comes, fear and anxiety are not coupled with it.

Go to Blue Letter Bible and look at the word *drought*. What is the very first definition that's given in Gesenius' Hebrew-Chaldee Lexicon?

_____

Is your brain tickling back to Day 2 of this week? And restraining your feet from even stepping foot on the path of sinners? When you restrain your feet from the way of the ones who miss the way, the restraint of water won't phase your roots because they are tapped into their own water source.

The path of sinners, as it turns out, is dry. Dusty. Entirely devoid of water. And, as a result, their roots are nothing more than withered weeds. Job 18:16 describes them perfectly. Write the verse here:

_____

_____

_____

The Living Bible takes it even further, describing the wicked as dead from the roots up because without any source of water, they cannot grow, which circles back around to the importance of a daily, habitual quiet time. You need to dig out those river channels to let your roots soak and spread out. When you don't make it a priority and set your quiet time aside, those waters start to recede—until they are entirely dried up.

Let's end our time together back in Psalm 1:3. What does the psalmist say about the blessed man's fruit?

If you explore the Hebrew word used for "that brings forth," you'll see a multidimensional picture of giving. The first qal-stem definition includes one last repeated phrase for our morning: "stretch out, extend." It's the opposite of withered and shriveled up. When your roots are shot out, spread out, and stretched out strong, your branches will stretch out the same, producing the kind of fruit that naturally comes from being soaked in the Word of God.

And that's the sweetest fruit there is.

DAY 6

PSALM 1:3C

This study is one that goes hand in hand with Job. Not the finer details of those deep-vein mines or the view of dug-out precious things, but the zoomed-out, bigger-picture version of Job's story. The one where he was stripped of everything he owned and loved.

Something similar happened to Joseph, only it was his brothers who sold him out of pure jealousy. But before we go there, let's read Psalm 1 again in its entirety.

How does God show His favor toward those who delight in His Word, according to the very end of Psalm 1:3? Whatever he does _____.

Hop on over to the first book of the Bible and read Genesis 39:1-23. What is the one thing that both the master and the prison keeper recognized about Joseph in verses 3 and 23?

Over and over, Joseph prospered. But he didn't just prosper by himself, in his own strength or efforts. He didn't prosper because of his charm or charisma. He prospered *because the Lord was with him.*

There's an interesting detail in the way the Hebrew is written. Not in the word descriptions or deeper definitions, but in the simple rendering of the original text.

Go to Blue Letter Bible and search for Genesis 39:3. Click on the Interlinear tool. Compare the column containing the English (KJV) words with the column of the Root Transliterated (Hebrew) by writing them side by side below:

English (KJV)	Root Form (Hebrew)

Did you notice that the same Hebrew word is used for the phrases "that the LORD" and "was with him, and that the LORD"? The reason Joseph prospered is not that his slave master and his prison keeper saw a shining example of a man in some very unfair circumstances. He prospered because they looked at Joseph *and saw the Lord.*

His master saw Jehovah. And, in turn, Jehovah made all that Joseph did to prosper.

Take a look at the phrase "made all that he did." First, what is the parsing information?

STEM: _____

ASPECT: _____

Do you remember the importance of the active participle aspect from page 92? What kind of action is it?

_____

Now, click on the Strong's link (H6213) for the phrase "made all that he did," keeping the proper stem in mind. What is the very first definition that's given in Gesenius' Hebrew-Chaldee Lexicon?

_____

_____

_____

Every single thing that Joseph put his hand to prospered. And the Hebrew word that's used for *to prosper* means to not only accomplish prosperously but *to finish well.* To stand unwavering in conviction and character like Joseph did—though he was sold out to slavery and bound innocent in prison. To refuse to let go of God, like Job did—though he was stripped of everything and suffered tremendously. Because He makes everything beautiful in His time (Ecclesiastes 3), and His ways are always strong and prospering (Psalm 10:5).

So restrain your feet from the way of sinners, because the way of God is prosperous. Just look at the way Joseph's story ended (he ended up running the entire country of Egypt). Or Job's (God blessed the end of his life more than the beginning). Hang on tight with white-knuckle faith, adhering to Psalm 1:1 and finishing well—even when it's tough.

And in the end, when people look at you they will see Jehovah. And you, tucked away somewhere inside, delighting in Him.

DAY 7

PSALM 1:4-6

Welcome back! We've made it to the end of our week together in Psalm 1, with roots pressed down deep, spread out, and soaking in the river channels of God's Word. With fruit hanging, leaves unwithered, and the favor of God upon us. Prospering us.

As beautiful and warm as the feeling is, we also have to face the stark reality of the flip side of the coin. Because, as the psalmist writes, the ungodly are not so. Their way is not the way of God, and their outcome is bleak. And though it might seem that they profit now, their way is nowhere near prosperous in the long run.

Read Psalm 1 in its entirety for the final time in our study, then write a brief synopsis of the ungodly based on verses 4-6 here:

_____

_____

_____

_____

_____

Do you remember Job's description of the roots of the wicked in Job 18:16? The ones that are dried out below and wither above? There is no life left to hang onto anything. Nothing to root into. So it makes sense that they blow away at the first gust of wind. They are like chaff.

Go to Blue Letter Bible, search for Psalm 1:4, and open the "Dictionaries" tool. Scroll down to _Vine's Expository Dictionary of New Testament Words_, and click on the link for _chaff._ How is chaff described?

_____

_____

_____

The chaff is the dead part of the grain—the part without weight or worth. It's the only part of the grain that's useless. And because of that, chaff people will not stand among the godly in judgment. It's interesting when you think about it. The blessed man who does not stand in the path of sinners will also not stand alongside them before God in heaven.

There are two different Hebrew words used for each instance of *stand* in Psalm 1. The first speaks of "remain or abide." And the second means "to arise, rise up, or stand up," as the guilty party does in a courtroom when the judge walks in, prepared to deliver the sentence.

These verses are a really good example of when I turn to a commentary for further insight, and Matthew Henry explains verse five this way:

> There is a judgment to come, in which every man's present character and work, though ever so artfully concealed and disguised, shall be truly and perfectly discovered, and appear in their own colours, and accordingly every man's future state will be, by an irreversible sentence, determined for eternity. The ungodly must appear in that judgment, to receive according to the things done in the body. They may hope to come off, nay, to come off with honour, but their hope will deceive them: *They shall not stand in the judgment,* so plain will the evidence be against them and so just and impartial will the judgment be upon it.[3]

The ungodly will be separated from the blessed men and women who finished well, continually restraining their feet and spreading out their roots. And the missed-the-way sinners will be apart from the congregation of the righteous. So it bodes us well to separate ourselves now in the pattern of Psalm 1:1 so that we will be found with the wheat instead of the chaff later.

Let's finish out our week strong with Psalm 1. Dig in deep to each word of verse six. Cross-reference and chew on the insight and meditate on God's truth, so that when the storm winds blow, they don't carry us off with them.

May your roots be well watered, and may they not dry up.

May your leaves be unwithered and evergreen.

And may you finish every day well. Prosperous, accomplished, and blessed.

Rest: A Word Study

Before we get into the how-to portion of this sample study, I want to take a minute to talk about the difference between a *word study* and a *topical study*. In general, topical studies seem to be a more popular method of Bible study, but they also are much too broad for my taste.

For example, if you're looking to do a topical Bible study on modern-day stress, you would look up multiple keywords that are associated with it. Words like *anxious*, *worry*, *fear*, or *burden*. Then you would take those words and look at their respective definitions and all of the references of their use in the Scripture.

Now that you know the way I study, that's a whole lot of information to track down and way too many treasure trails to follow. Because of that, I prefer to do a word study—a much more specific and detailed look at a particular word—over a general idea.

Because even just one English word can have multiple translations in the biblical languages, word studies can be just as robust as topical themes. And, as you'll see, just as rich.

Rest. It's a word that stirred in my quiet-time waters for quite some time, showing up in the form of cross-references and unexpected conviction. You know the feeling—that heaviness that comes with knowing that you need to do something in order to be obedient to God.

That was rest for me a few years ago. I had settled into a new routine of staying instead of leaving. Remaining at home rather than traveling.

All of my favorite photography friends were gathering at the Ritz-Carlton in Georgia for an annual retreat that I hadn't missed in six years. This year, I had been invited to speak. But I turned down the speaking engagement and the opportunity to mentor. I chose to stay home.

A handful of weeks prior, I had come across a handful of words attributed to Mother Teresa that marked the beginning of God tucking back my hair to whisper-reveal the word that would be my theme for that year: "If you want to bring happiness to the whole world, go home and love your family," she said. Later, I had the words scripted onto a piece of wood that still hangs in the entry of our home as a daily reminder to stay.

For eight years, I averaged a trip somewhere every ten weeks. Napa, Vail, Scottsdale, Dallas, Whistler, Atlanta, Paris. Weekends with girlfriends, teaching, traveling for clients, and traveling with clients. I relished it all. And, on some level, it filled that ever-present family void. In 2015 alone, I flew nearly 60,000 miles. And out of half a dozen off-island trips, Josh was only with me on *one* of them.

But that year? It was time to settle in, stay home, and learn to say no. That year, I resolved to travel more *with* my husband than without him. And when we were home, I vowed to be doing a lot of that.

As women created to live and breathe in an increasingly impatient, go-after-it generation, where hustle is habit and empires are envied, I wanted to know what it really, truly looked like to rest in the Lord. I wanted to learn how to reset the habit of hustle. To ease up on the jam-packed schedule. And to quiet my hurried and anxious brain.

I wanted rest to be my new hustle. So I started to dig.

And that is where we will pick things up together—right there at the beginning.

THE REST RESEARCH

Go to www.blueletterbible.org and type the word *rest* into the search bar. You'll see right away that we have a little bit of work ahead of us. How many times does *rest* occur in the KJV, and in how many verses?

Clearly, rest is an important theme in Scripture. When I saw those numbers, I knew I had to put in a little bit of legwork to categorize all those occurrences and be able to see the bigger picture a little bit better.

MAKE A TALLIED LIST

Take some time to click through every single reference individually. You can ignore all references to *rest* as an amount, such as "the rest of the people" or "the rest of the acts of the king." That will help to narrow down the results from 275 to 134.

While you dig around, make a list of every new word you encounter on the lines below. Then, as words are repeated, you can add a tick mark next to the corresponding word on your list. This will allow you to see the most often-used words and the rarer instances that might pique your interest. Also, if you come across a verse in your digging that resonates with you personally, feel free to include the reference in your list.

This is the most time-consuming part of doing a word study, and it's okay to break this into a couple of different days if you need to.

HEBREW

1. _____

2. _____

3. _____

4. _____

5. _____

6. _____

7. _____

8. _____

9. _____

10. _____

11. _____

12. _____

13. _____

14. _____

15. _____

16. _____

17. _____

18. _____

19. _____

20. _____

21. _____

22. _____

23. _____

24. _____

25. _____

GREEK

1. _____

2. _____

3. _____

4. _____

5. _____

6. _____

7. _____

8. _____

9. _____

10. _____

Whew! You did it! Those initial 275 results in 265 verses are now a much more manageable 35 words. We could easily spend the rest of the year digging into this curated list and chasing down those glorious treasure trails. But for this sample study, we'll only look at a small handful.

MAKE A PLAN

Now that you have a narrowed-down list of every instance of *rest* in the Bible, it's time to make a plan for digging into the results of your research. To do that, go back and highlight the following items in your list:

- the first occurrence of *rest*
- the last occurrence of *rest*
- the most repeated words for both Hebrew and Greek (hint: there might be a tie between two different words)
- the most popular references (the ones that you can recite after reading the first couple of words because they're well known and well loved)
- one or two that resonated with you

Yes, it took some legwork, but with a little bit of research and a small amount of planning, you now have a good handful of words and verses to dig into in a pre-planned stretch of systematic study days for your quiet time.

Tomorrow, we will begin digging into those neatly formed *rest* word piles. But today? I want you to wrap up your time here putting pen to prayer journal paper. Take some time to pray about the kind of rest you're craving. Is it rest from work? Travel? Striving? Maybe you're looking to rest from the hustle. Or you want to take a breather from worry or anxiety or overthinking. Whatever it is, pray it out honest before God. And tomorrow, we'll fill that emptied-out space with some dug-out treasures of truth.

See you then!

DAY 2
REST AT FIRST MENTION

Welcome back! I'm so glad that you're on this resting journey with me, and I can't wait to start digging into those words we highlighted together yesterday.

You might have heard somewhere along the way about the importance of the first mention of something in the Bible. Whether it's a word like *light*, *blood*, *worship*, or *love*, the very first time a doctrinal theme is encountered in Scripture is a very big deal. This is called The Rule of First Mention, and it says that the first mention of a concept is the simplest and clearest presentation of it, essentially laying the foundation for every other mention to then build upon it.

As you might imagine, most (if not all) of the most important biblical concepts are first mentioned in Genesis, and *rest* is no different. But finding the real first mention of the word can be tricky, depending upon which translation you use.

If you go according to the KJV, the first mention of *rest* is in Genesis 8:9, when Noah had been stranded in the ark and floating on a flooded earth for just over six months. He had no inclination as to when (if ever) he would get off that boat, when the waters started to slowly recede. A couple more months went by when he sent out that dove, trying to find some hope of dry ground to return to.

Spoiler alert #1: If you look into the Hebrew word that's used for *rest* in Genesis 8:9, there are a couple of different references, and they all include a similar pattern: looking for rest and *not* finding it.

Spoiler alert #2: That wasn't exactly what I was looking for.

I switched the default KJV translation to the NKJV. And it turns out that *rest* in the KJV is translated *resting* in the NKJV. So I moved along to the new first mention of simple four-letter *rest*. As soon as I read it, I knew I was getting somewhere.

Go to Genesis 18. Read verses 1-8, then write verse 4 here:

_____

_____

_____

Next, go to Genesis 18:4 on Blue Letter Bible and open the Interlinear tools. Before clicking on the Strong's word, take note of the "parse" button. What is the proper parsing of the Hebrew word for "and rest yourselves"?

STEM: _____

ASPECT: _____

Click on the Strong's link (H8172) and write the definition of the word from the Outline of Biblical Usage here (hint: Make sure you're looking at the correct stem):

_____

_____

_____

For a more detailed description of the word, read the full entry that's included under Gesenius' Hebrew-Chaldee Lexicon, and write anything that sparks your interest here:

_____

_____

_____

Now, we're going to piece all of that together with the context of the story. We find our first mention of rest as Abraham sits in the door of his tent at the hottest part of the day when God appeared to him. What did Abraham do first?

_____

Abraham ran to meet God that day. The moment he recognized the Lord standing there with those three men, Abraham ran to Him and bowed down. Then he uttered our first-mention reference. What did Abraham invite God and His three companions to do?

In the middle of the day, when the work was far from being finished, Abraham was likely taking a quick break from the running and the doing and the everyday hustle. And Sarah was busy inside cooking and cleaning and finishing chores. Abraham invited God into the chaos of it all. To not just sit, but to recline there in the shade of the terebinth trees with him.

When I imagine a perfect day of rest, it involves a spa robe and lying down for a massage before finishing the afternoon reclined poolside with an ice-cold drink and a really good book. But this first mention of rest turns everything that I associate with the idea on its head. Biblical rest does not begin with *me* lying down and taking a deep breath. True biblical rest begins with inviting God into the chaos of my day. Asking Him to sit awhile with me while I hasten to prepare my heart for Him and hustle to holiness. Rest begins with asking God to interrupt the work and the distractions and the day-to-day monotony, then choosing to sit down and rest-recline with Him.

Head on over to Luke 10:38-42 for a Scripture-explaining-Scripture story of one woman's rest in action, starkly contrasted with another's action without rest. According to Jesus in verse 42, whose choice was the better one?

Before we go, there's one more thing I want you to take note of. Go back to Genesis 18 and read verse 10. What promise did God give Abraham that day?

In this first mention of *rest*, after Abraham chooses the better part of hastening to holiness and invites God to interrupt his day, that is when God chooses to speak His promise. When He is reclined there under the tree, that is the moment God tells Abraham of the long-awaited miracle.

As Mark Batterson puts it, "You never know when or where or how God will invade the routine of your life."[1] But you can know this: It always starts with rest.

DAY 3
TAKING A CAMEL REST

We kicked off our word study on *rest* yesterday by looking at the very first occurrence of the word in Scripture, and it probably wasn't what you thought it would be. It wasn't that God past-tense *rested* on the seventh day after creating the entire world, or that Noah's dove could not find a *resting* place for her feet after the flood. It's plain and simple recline-under-a-tree *rest*.

To a lot of us, *rest* might seem like a forbidden four-letter word. But those four simple letters usher in God's promise—right there in the midst of the hustle and the chores. When the breakfast dishes are still in the sink as dinner time nears, when emails need answering and deadlines are looming, when social media demands more of you than you really have to offer, *rest* is asking God to sit awhile with you in the middle of it all. And then inviting His Spirit to remain with you while you finish your work.

Today we're going to look at a more topographical list. We're going to study the most popular Hebrew word. According to the word list you made, what is the one word that's used most consistently out of the 25 renditions for *rest* in the Old Testament?

Go to Blue Letter Bible and open Joshua 3:13. In the Interlinear tab, find the phrase *shall rest*. Before clicking on the Strong's word, take note of the "parse" button. What is the proper parsing of the Hebrew word for *shall rest*?

STEM: _____

ASPECT: _____

Click on the Strong's number (H5117) to look at the word a little more closely. According to the KJV Translation Count, how many times is the word *nuwach* used? _____

And how many times is that word translated as *rest?* _____

Click on the link for "rest (55x)" inside the KJV Translation Count box, and skim through the list of concordance results. I've chosen a few key verses below. Read through each one and give a simple summary of the kind of rest that is described.

Joshua 3:13 _____

_____

Exodus 10:14 _____

_____

Exodus 20:11 _____

_____

Proverbs 14:33 _____

_____

Ezekiel 44:30 _____

_____

Joshua 1:13, 15 _____

_____

Nuwach speaks of resting the soles of your feet like the priests did in the book of Joshua, right before God stopped up the river so they could walk through dry. It speaks of the ark resting on Mount Ararat in Genesis 8:4. It's the ark of the covenant resting after searching out a resting place for the people in Numbers 10:33-36. And it's the Spirit of the Lord resting upon the people.

It speaks of the Sabbath day rest and the people resting from their enemies in Esther 9:22. It speaks of wisdom resting at home in an understanding heart, and the blessing that rests on the house of the person who gives firstfruits to the Lord. It speaks of the rest that God gives: rest from sorrow (Isaiah 14:3), rest from enemies (Deuteronomy 12:10), and rest in His presence (Exodus 33:14).

Nuwach speaks of the Levitical priests depositing their most holy garments—worn only in the inner court of the tabernacle—away for safekeeping (Ezekiel 42:14). Of laying things up and laying them out before the Lord (Deuteronomy 26:10). Of leaving people alone and undisturbed (or not, as the case may be) (Esther 3:8). But out of all those things, there is *one* kind of *nuwach* rest that piqued my interest. Only one that fit the kind of rest I was searching for.

Go back to the Strong's page for *nuwach* and view the full entry from Gesenius' Hebrew-Chaldee Lexicon. Remember the parsing information that you noted a few minutes ago? Because the qal stem is specified, you know that you are really only paying attention to the first two paragraphs in the lexicon entry that are specific to that stem.

What is the very first definition for *nuwach*?

_____

_____

_____

That's the kind of rest I was looking for. The kind that sits down for a minute like Abraham was doing in the doorway of his tent that time that God appeared to him. But if you read a little bit further, the lexicon has an even more specific example of the type of rest *nuwach* describes, pulling from the Arabic rendition of the word: "to kneel down as a camel; a place where camels lie down."

What is it about camels? I thought. *Why are they mentioned specifically?* I started digging around and doing some research when I came across a book from 1875. In it was a description of camel rest: "Some writers claim that the resting posture of the camel is a thing taught him by his master for his own convenience...We are aware that a camel has to be trained to kneel down or rise up at the word of command...But we have never seen a camel resting otherwise, whether old or young, not even the new-born foal."[2]

The author went on to describe domesticated elephants that are trained to kneel first, then lie down (the same way camels do). But in the wild? Camels take their rest leaning against a tree. They have to be trained to lie down when they rest. Forced, even, by their handlers tying ropes around their legs and pulling down their necks and applying downward pressure on their hindquarters. It's a posture of rest that comes about only by training.

And all at once, the words of Psalm 23 came flooding into my mind.

Read Psalm 23, and then write verses 1-3a here:

_____

_____

_____

_____

Camels can endure the desert. They can withstand scorching temperatures and survive upward of ten days without water in the scorching heat. They can walk 30 miles a day, carrying 800 pounds on their backs, for several days in a row without needing a break. Camels are strong, perfectly dependable, and entirely capable of bearing burdens in the most extreme circumstances.

Isn't that how we feel as women today? The Jill-of-all-trades who wears many hats and juggles marriage, career, and motherhood simultaneously? Striving to be that Proverbs

31 woman who can do it all without asking for help? We want to check off the list without taking a breath, to be intimate with our husbands, intentional with our physical children, and influential to our spiritual ones. And all the while, skyrocketing our way to the top as a driven, failure-is-not-an-option, I-am-my-own-boss, the-world-is-my-oyster, twenty-first-century woman. *It ain't no thang.*

But just because you are strong, perfectly dependable and entirely capable doesn't mean that taking a little bit of time to sit down, breathe, and rest is detrimental. And it certainly doesn't show weakness. And it doesn't mean that the momentum you've worked so hard for will suddenly be interrupted.

Camels were created to be resilient. But somewhere along the way, a camel-herdsman decided that training his animal to rest was in both their best interests. He decided that his camel might be *that much more effective* at what it was created to do if a little bit of rest was forced.

Friends, let's allow God to be our herdsman. To lead us beside the still waters. To train us to lie down.

In case you're like me and need the actual tie back to Psalm 23 and not just a vague "this reminds me of" phrase, here's a little lifeline: The Hebrew word used for *still* or *quiet* waters in Psalm 23:2? It's one of the 25 Hebrew words for *rest*.

Let's end our time together with a prayer pulled from the dug-out words of Psalm 23:

LORD, You are my herdsman. There is nothing that I am lacking. When I start to think that I am perfectly capable of getting through my day or chasing my dream or finding success without You, Lord, interrupt me. Force me to lie down in pastures of tender grass. Lead me to a watering place by quiet, restful waters to be refreshed so that I can be an excellent woman, wife, mother, and friend. Give me rest at the resting-place waters. Train me to build this rest into my day, if only for a few minutes. For Your name's sake, amen.

DAY 4

THE PLACE OF CANAAN REST

Today, we're going to set aside our camel rest in favor of some Canaan rest, and leave the Old Testament to dig into the New Testament occurrences of *rest*. I hinted during your research at the possibility of a tie between two Greek words for the most common usage, and we will begin with one of them. Take a look back at the list you made. What were the two Greek words most commonly used for *rest*?

We've spent the last two days looking at rest as a verb. But we also want to consider what it looks like when we take our rest-in-action to the noun of our rest. Enter *katapausis* and the chock-full-of-rest section of Hebrews 3 and 4.

Open your Bible and read Hebrews 3:1–4:11. Did you notice how many times the word *rest* is mentioned? It's repeated ten times in 21 verses, and seven of those instances are *katapausis* rest. (If you've adopted my color-coding system, now is the time to grab that orange pen and start circling!)

According to Hebrews 4:1, what is the promise that still stands for us today?

In Genesis 18, Abraham rested with God before the promise. And in Hebrews 4, God's place of rest *is* the promise.

The definition of *katapausis* is multifaceted. Use Blue Letter Bible to look up the Strong's tools for the word *rest* in Hebrews 4:1. What are the definitions according to the Outline of Biblical Usage?

I. _____

   A. _____

II. _____

   A. _____

Did that second definition catch your eye? *Calming of the winds.* Putting the doubts and the chaos and the storm to rest—just like those calmed winds you just studied in Psalm 107. A calming of the winds isn't necessarily a place, but if you look back at Psalm 107, God *did* take those men who were at the end of themselves somewhere after He calmed the storm. Where does verse 30 say He took them?

_____

As an aside, read that verse side by side with Psalm 37:1-7, which happens to hold another Old Testament occurrence of rest and God-given desires of the heart. And they happen to also be coupled with trusting in Him. Delighting in Him. *Resting in Him.*

But let's get back to *katapausis* and that last definition you just wrote down. The one describing a metaphorical picture of heaven and that blessed promise of forever rest in the place where He forever dwells. After we persevere and jump the hurdles and run our race, after the toils and trials are finished, the light affliction that lasted just a moment will lead to that eternal weight of glory.

It's a glorious dichotomy, when you think about it. "Come to Me," Jesus says when He sees us breathless and exhausted from work and worry. "Let Me take that weight off of you." And He trades out our heavy burdens for His light and easy yoke, giving beauty for ashes, the oil of joy for mourning, and the garment of praise for the spirit of heaviness.

That trade enables us to run our race another day. Despite the diagnosis, or the stress of a strong-willed child, or the heartbreak of delayed fertility, or the wait of an unfulfilled dream. Despite every single thing that threatens to steal our rest, we run our race another day...and another day after that, and one more after that. And then, when it's all said and done, when we stand before Him in that heavenly rest, He takes back His light and easy yoke. And returns to us a different kind of weight. One that is, somehow, weightless.

But we can't forget the original Old Testament place of rest. It was the land God promised the Israelites, the Canaan that they craved when they wandered in the desert for those 40 years. That's what God is referring to in that concentrated use of *katapausis* in Hebrews. During that 40-year stretch, God was actually angry with the Israelites, and they couldn't enter His Canaan rest. According to Hebrews 3:19, why couldn't the wilderness wanderers enter Canaan?

We talk so much these days about being exhausted—about wanting a break and needing to learn to rest. But the fundamental truth is that we will only experience true rest through Jesus.

God promised that unbelieving generation of Israelites a land of rest. It was right there, and it was theirs for the taking. But they fell short because they didn't believe Him.

God promised believing Abraham a son. And though it took quite a while, he did not waver in unbelief. He was strengthened in faith, and God counted him righteous.

Is there something in your life that you're struggling to believe God's promise for? Something that's causing you to waver in the wait?

LORD, may we not miss out on Your promise of rest because we refuse to believe You. Oh, God, help our unbelief. And help us to hope in heaven and the promise of Your katapausis *place of rest.*

DAY 5
THE SOCIETY HUSTLE

Hello, friend! I cannot wait to dig into today's study with you. But first, let's do a quick recap on the last few days. So far we've looked at three different kinds of rest in Scripture:

- Abraham inviting God into his hustle to rest upon His elbow and stay for a while (the first occurrence of *rest* in the Old Testament)
- The trained rest of camels that isn't necessarily vital but is always welcome (the most popular Hebrew word for rest)
- The promise of rest and the prerequisite of unwavering faith (one of the most-used Greek words for rest)

Today, we're going to look at the other tied-for-most-common Greek word: *anapauō*. Open your Bible and read Matthew 11:28-30 to find the first occurrence of the word *rest* in the New Testament (it should be familiar to you already since we looked at it together back in chapter five). Write verse 28 here:

_____

_____

_____

Go to Blue Letter Bible and open Matthew 11:28, then click on the Interlinear tab. Find the word *rest* and click on the Strong's number (G373) to do some digging. You will see under the Root Word (Etymology) section that *anapauō* is a compound of two different Greek words. Click on each, and write the word as well as its basic definition here:

1. _____

2. _____

Now, combine the two words together to form a loose translation of *anapauō*:

_____

Next, go back to the Strong's page for *anapauō*. What is the first definition listed under the Outline of Biblical Usage?

_____

_____

_____

Now that you have a solid foundation of the meaning of *anapauō*, let's take a peek at the KJV concordance results to see where else the word is used in the New Testament. Read through these verses and give a simple summary of the rest that is described, just like you did yesterday:

Revelation 14:13 _____

_____

1 Peter 4:14 _____

_____

1 Corinthians 16:18 _____

_____

Mark 6:31 _____

_____

Anapauō not only speaks of causing someone to cease or desist from movement or labor in order to recover and collect strength, it also speaks of the blessed rest of the dead and the kind of rest that only comes in heaven. It speaks of the Spirit of God resting upon you, moving and motivating you to act a certain way. It speaks of deep-soul refreshment.

And it speaks of rest after traveling.

Considering the events that got the ball rolling on this entire study of rest, these words piqued my interest. And that one little tidbit in Mark 6 was, by far, the most interesting application of *anapauō* rest that I encountered. The one in verse 31 that describes the twelve men that Jesus handpicked to be the closest to Him. They had been sent out as missionaries in pairs of two and they took nothing with them when they left. No walking sticks to ease the journey. No food. No extra change of clothes. Not even money.

The men all went out in different directions, bare-bones traveling. Preaching. And anointing, healing, performing miracles. And then, when they had done all that they could, they came back home.

The missionaries were all together again for the first time in Mark 6, sharing their stories of what God had done and the miracles that had happened, when Jesus interrupted the excited conversation. A lot of people needed them, and He told them to rest a while. Because even the most effective men and women in ministry need a little down time.

Those people that the disciples were serving while Jesus was teaching? They were in a constant state of hurry. They were coming and going and not even taking time to eat—all the signs of a textbook case of the hustle.

Use Blue Letter Bible to look at the definitions for both coming and going in Mark 6:31.

COMING: _____

GOING: _____

The people were showing up in multitudes to make appearances. To try to find their place of influence. Wanting to be known. And then almost sinking out of sight when they couldn't find their place—politely dismissed without noise or notice.

If that doesn't describe today's social media rat race, I don't know what does. The desire to find your place and take your platform. To see and be seen. To tag and comment and strategically align yourself in a way that carves out your place of influence. And to become known by the number of followers you have.

And then, in those overwhelming "nothing I'm doing is working" moments? Or those moments of comparison and jealousy as you sit back and watch the coming and the going? The ones that make you want to slink away with your tail between your legs, discouraged and embarrassed because your house isn't Pinterest-worthy, your selfie isn't perfectly posed, you don't have a vacation in sight, and their grass looks greener than yours? It's in those moments that you log out without noise or notice. Until you log back in and the vicious cycle starts all over again.

That, my friends, is the hustle. It's a merry-go-round of striving, exhaustion, and comparison. And Jesus sees it a mile away. He recognized the always-on exhaustion of the disciples who were serving the multitude. He invited them to rest, right there in the midst of the normal society hustle.

Whether you're serving, caught up in the hustle, or maybe a little bit of both, the invitation is still the same:

> Come to me. Get away with me and you'll recover your life. I'll show you how to take a real rest. Walk with me and work with me—watch how I do it. Learn the unforced rhythms of grace. I won't lay anything heavy or ill-fitting on you. Keep company with me and you'll learn to live freely and lightly (Matthew 11:28-30 MSG).

I don't know about you, but I'll take that over the hustle any day of the week.

DAY 6
REST BEFORE THE MIRACLE

We're going to linger a little bit longer in Mark 6 today. There's another aspect of that *anapauō* rest that I want you to see. But before we get to that, let's head over one book and read Matthew's account of the same story. His version of the story brings one detail to light that Mark's leaves out. It happens just before Jesus' invitation to rest, and it's found in Matthew 14:1-12.

What is the basic summary of those 12 verses?

_____

_____

_____

What did Jesus do after He heard of Herod's dinner party in verse 13?

_____

Jesus wasn't only recognizing the disciples' need to get away for a minute to rest. He was recognizing His own. He had just lost a good friend, and I imagine the grief was just as real in that moment as it was in John 11 when He wept after Lazarus died.

Write Jesus' words from Mark 6:31 here:

_____

Where did Jesus invite the travel-weary men to go?

_____

Some translations use the phrase "deserted place." Others say "quiet place." But the KJV renders it *desert place*. And the Greek word that Jesus uses means it's solitary, lonely, and desolate, in both location and population. It's a wilderness area that is (usually) entirely devoid of others—particularly friends, family, and acquaintances.

Jesus invited the travel-weary missionary men to go with Him to a solitary and deserted place to rest awhile. Not for long. A small amount of time—just enough to catch their breath and then get back to work again.

But by the time they arrived, five thousand people were there waiting for them. And a miracle was about to go down.

Wait. Did you catch that? *A miracle was about to go down.* A miracle of divided and devoured fish, of broken and multiplied bread loaves.

But first, Jesus rested with His disciples.

Do you see a pattern emerging? Think back to the most-used Hebrew word. The one that was used when Abraham was about to receive the miracle-answer to his 20-year-long prayer.

But first, he rested.

And now, five thousand people were about to dine on a dinner made for one.

But first, the weary miracle workers rested.

Ann Voskamp was elbow-deep in bread dough when she realized it:

> I shape loaves and think how Jesus took the bread and gave thanks…and then the miracle of the multiplying of the loaves and the fish.
>
> How Jesus took the bread and gave thanks…and then the miracle of Jesus enduring the cross for the joy set before Him.
>
> How Jesus stood outside Lazarus's tomb, the tears streaming down His face, and He looked up and prayed, "Father, thank you that you have heard me" (John 11:41 NIV). And then the miracle of a dead man rising! Thanksgiving raises the dead!
>
> …How there is thanks…and then the mind-blowing miracle! I lay loaves into pans and feel years of the angst lying down too.
>
> *Eucharisteo*—thanksgiving—*always precedes the miracle.*[3]

But you know what? Thankfulness isn't the only thing that precedes miracles.

Rest does too.

But what happens when the miracle doesn't come and the wait drags on? What happens when the dove finds no place to rest her feet, and you're just stuck there, still on that ark, waiting? Let's circle back to a verse I mentioned in passing a couple of days ago. The one in Psalm 37.

What does the first part of Psalm 37:7 say?

Sometimes, there is rest in the waiting because there's nothing else you can do *but* rest and wait.

The root of the Hebrew word that's used for *rest* is onomatopoeic. It's an imitation of the sound of a shut mouth. And it literally means "to cease astonishment." You know how you can get so worked up because you can't believe what's happened? When you can't stop talking about it—even though there's nothing you can actually *do* about it?

In those moments, David says that we need to shut our mouths, stop talking, and quietly, confidently, *patiently* wait for the Lord.

Buried deep in the definition of that Hebrew word is a cross-reference to the Noah story and the dove without a resting place for her feet. It's easy to assume that the flood only lasted for 40 days. But really, the rain only lasted that long. It would be another 335 days before that family walked off that ark.

Imagine—almost a year of wanting nothing more than to stand on dry ground. Almost a year of sitting in the ark, waiting for that season to be over. Waiting for the lessons to be learned and the message to be a memory. But all they could do was shut their mouths and rest in the wait. They had no other choice but to rest on God until that ark rested on that mountain.

And then, when it finally did, they walked right on out of there with an olive leaf in hand and a rainbow in the sky and a mighty, miraculous story to tell.

So today, if you're resting in anticipation of a miracle, invite God to Abraham-rest with you. And David-rest quietly. Wait patiently. And remind yourself of Spurgeon's timeless words: "Time is nothing to Him; let it be nothing to thee."[4]

Epilogue

The beginning of 2016 happened to coincide with the beginning of a brand-new prayer journal. I stood staring at shelves of journals in the bookstore one afternoon, taking in my array of options, when one cover caught my eye. It was ornate where I typically choose plain and featured an intricately illustrated tree that immediately brought two words to mind: *family tree.*

I picked it up and ran my hand over the soft leather. *Maybe this journal will be the one,* I thought. *The one with the theme of answered prayer and promise fulfilled and miracle rendered.*

The year was already looking to be a year of finishing—finishing my list of 1,000 thanks, finishing my ten-year journey through *Search the Scriptures. Even if this journal is not those things,* I wrote just a few pages and days in, *it's still a chronicling of my daily conversations with You. Because rest and mundane and the same old thing is still okay. There is still glory there too.*

But the wait was getting to me.

The longer this stretches on, I prayed three weeks later, *the more out-of-control my emotions feel. And the more Josh and I fight. Loud, dramatic, and painful words spoken and then not-talking-for-days kind of fights. I feel like a rabid dog, growling and baring my teeth and gnashing at his gentle hands held out to comfort.*

Lord, how much longer? I scratched over the letters again, making them bold. *Where is Your miracle? My eyes have been on You. Over and over, I have reminded myself that it is well with me. I have stared into caves and stared down mountains and given* eucharisteo *thanks. I've long anticipated the miracle. And still, almost 120 months later, it hasn't come. Tears drip off my nose and I whisper again: It is nothing for You!*

I grabbed my Bible and it fell open to Psalm 107, with the sailors and the storm and the towering waves:

> You shot high in the sky, then the bottom dropped out;
> > your hearts were stuck in your throats.
> You were spun like a top, you reeled like a drunk,
> > you didn't know which end was up.
> Then you called out to GOD in your desperate condition;
> > he got you out in the nick of time.
> He quieted the wind down to a whisper,
> > put a muzzle on all the big waves.
> And you were so glad when the storm died down,
> > and he led you safely back to harbor.
> So thank GOD for his marvelous love,
> > for his miracle mercy to the children he loves.
> > > Psalm 107:23-32 MSG

Sometimes the miracle lies in the emotional storm surge subsiding, I wrote. *And sometimes, the miracle is simply His mercy.*

Sometimes, the miracle is simply His mercy.

Then February came.

I was early in the study on rest when I saw the first occurrence of it. The one right there in Genesis with God and Abraham and His promise for their family. The rest that came before the miracle.

It was Groundhog Day, which was always a little representative of every month for me. But that month marked our ten-year anniversary of delayed fertility. Not infertility—that word never sat right with me. So I called it *delayed* instead. We had spent ten years waiting for our miracle. Ten years of pounding fists on heaven's walls, and wrestling with sovereignty, and learning obedience. Ten years of stretched faith and endless tears. Ten years of swinging between hope and sorrow, and recalling that deeply-rooted promise that *nothing* is impossible for Him.

I commemorated it with a more-honest-than-I-had-ever-been post on social media.

> It feels silly to say out loud, but more than once I've wondered: *Are we doing it wrong?* And then there are the days when I think the same about my faith. *Is it not enough?*
>
> I have learned through carefully studied body language who I can truly share the struggle with and who I can't. Because the second the topic of conversation goes there, and eye contact is broken, and hands are fiddled with, I pull my head back into my shell and gently steer things back to more safe waters. The ones that are far away from the *I can't get pregnant and God has asked us to wait* pool.
>
> Whether you've tried for ten months or ten years, infertility is the worst kind of heartache. But the companion to that? Without it, I wouldn't have the marriage that I do. And without my story? The one of loss and waiting and delayed fertility? I wouldn't know God the way that I do. I wouldn't have an insatiable hunger for His Word because it's the *only* thing that has kept me afloat.

And then there was March.

I was in the middle of my normal quiet-time routine, reading in the book of Daniel, when I felt the sudden urge to pick up that beloved *Streams in the Desert* devotional. It had been more than three years since I had read it last. After Shawna died, I just sort of...stopped.

But on that Wednesday morning, I opened it afresh. And the verse for the day was a familiar one. David was praying God's promise:

So now, O LORD, may the promise You made about your servant and his family become a permanent reality! Do as You promised, so it may become a reality and You may gain lasting fame, as people say, "The LORD who commands armies is the God of Israel." David's dynasty will be established before You (1 Chronicles 17:23-24 NET).

I prayed the words as David prayed them after I finished re-reading the verses, remembering that other devotional promise God had given me for my own family.

Lord, I prayed, *do as You promised, so that the someday-words may be a reality, and that You may gain lasting fame, and that Your name may be magnified. Lord, please, do as You promised!*

And then I took a quick peek at the Living Bible's translation of the same verse. In the part where David said, "Do as You promised," the Living Bible reads, "I accept Your promise, Lord" (v. 23 TLB).

I loved the different translation and wrote it in my tree-adorned prayer journal. And then I went back to the devotional to read these words from F. B. Meyer: "Hardly any stance could be more completely beautiful, strong, or safe than that of putting your finger on a promise of God's divine Word and then claiming it. Doing so requires no anguish, struggle, or wrestling but simply presenting the check and asking for cash. It is as simple as producing the promise and claiming its fulfillment."[1]

They were interesting words. Words that I wanted to believe and act upon. But I was afraid I was reading too much into it and, once again, spinning God's Word to be applicable to what I *wanted* to hear. So I set the devotional aside and went back to my place in the book of Daniel to finish reading the chapter I had already started.

I read of Daniel's dreams and visions and then, one stand-out phrase: "Daniel kept the matter in his heart" (Daniel 7:28). I already knew the cross-reference that would be noted there without even having to look. It pointed to Luke 2:19, which was another verse that led me to another link in the family-promise chain that God had given me five years earlier.

Do you remember that restaurant lobby where Shawna slipped me that birthday gift? After I opened it, I was talking to another girlfriend as we waited for our table.

"I had a dream about you last night," she said. "I want to share it with you. Let's meet for coffee!"

I met Kristin the next evening. She told me that in her dream, she was standing backstage at a conference where I was teaching, holding a baby.

"Whose baby is that?" someone asked in the periphery.

"This is Josh and Jane's baby!" she told them proudly.

When Kristin shared the dream with me, she did so carefully, emphasizing that she did not know if I had birthed the child or how that baby came about. All she knew was it was *ours*.

I felt like Mary as I drove home that night, keeping it all and pondering it in my heart.

I felt like Mary as I drove home that night, keeping it all and pondering it in my heart. The words were so clear in my mind that the moment I got home, I pulled out my Bible and found the pondering words kept safe in Luke 2:19.

When I did, another verse on the facing page caught my eye. It was boxed out in pink and begging for attention. When I read the words, Holy-Spirit goose bumps covered my skin from head to toe:

> Blessed is she who believed, for there will be a fulfillment of those things which were told her from the Lord (Luke 1:45).

Remembering Kristin's dream, I came back to Daniel and 1 Chronicles 17. I sat there for a minute, chewing on it all. Then, trusting that all of the details that morning were not just a coincidence, I picked up my pen and prayed nervously but boldly, *Lord, DO AS YOU PROMISED. I accept Your promise. Fulfill Your word.*

TWO HOURS LATER, the balloon of hope dramatically deflated. My period had started four days early. I felt foolish. Disappointed. And embarrassed that I had rattled on, getting my hopes up again, for the one hundred twenty-first time.

I tried to remind myself that this is what faith is about. Asking and then asking again. Knocking, then knocking again. But I had been knocking endlessly without an answer to the door. And it was getting harder and harder to convince myself to go back and knock again, just one more time.

> *This is what faith is about. Asking and then asking again.*

TWO DAYS PASSED, and I was back at my typical morning perch, continuing on in my regular quiet-time routine. This time, I was in Daniel's ninth chapter. The angel Gabriel came to Daniel to tell him that at the very moment he was studying Scripture and began praying—at *that very moment*—a command was given as a direct answer to Daniel's prayer.

After reading and understanding Jeremiah's prophecies, Daniel boldly asked God for the captivity of his people to end. But he didn't ask for it sometime in the future. *Do it now*, he prayed.

Daniel had no idea at the time that God was acting on his prayer at the very moment he had prayed it.

But Gabriel did. And he was sent to Daniel to tell him about it.

"Daniel," he said, "you had no sooner started your prayer when the answer was given" (Daniel 9:22-23 MSG). When I read the words from The Message's translation, I breathed out deep.

Lord, I crave that, I poured it out honest. *I crave an end to all this waiting. I crave the answer given. I crave a dramatic movement of Your Spirit.*

And I left it at that. Because sometimes you need to acknowledge a deep yearning that just won't quit.

And then you have to trust that He heard you.

TWO DAYS AFTER that, I had our tiny home to myself. It was a rare Sunday that Josh had to work, and I was taking advantage of the time alone to catch up on some work of my own when I started thinking.

That period I thought had started four days earlier had never really kicked in.

*I wonder…*I thought.

Again, my curiosity got the best of me. So I took a pregnancy test, laid it on the counter, set the timer on my phone, and walked out of the bathroom to work for a couple of minutes. As I walked out, I glanced back. The results window was still blinding white. I shook my head, unsure of why I kept doing that to myself.

When the timer went off, I got up to throw the test away, deep in thought over a design project I was working on.

Then I saw it: two pink lines.

I'm not sure there are words adequate to really describe that moment. Shaking hands, a racing mind, buckling knees, and a heart much too scared to believe that it could ever really be true.

I fell on the floor and wept.

And stared at the pink lines.

And wept.

And stared and wept and stared and wept. When I finally had the wherewithal to move from the holy ground of that bathroom floor, I pulled myself up again to take another test.

This time, the double lines showed up almost instantly.

I grabbed my camera and photographed the first positive pregnancy test I had ever taken in my life, and I named the file "miracle.jpg" before putting it on a USB drive and driving to the store to print it at a photo kiosk. I picked out a frame and some simple wrapping and drove home to wrap it up tight.

I propped the wrapped-up photograph of the proof of our miracle on the coffee table, ready for Josh to find when he came home.

THE NEXT MORNING, I woke up and rolled over to look out the window at the barely dawn, soft gray light. I could only manage two words in my head: *It's over*.

I should have had something profound to say. But the overwhelming glory of the Lord had rendered me completely and utterly speechless.

As I lay there, I began to get curious about that period I thought had come early. So I did a quick search on my phone for "spotting day 24." My eyes grew wide when I read one of the first results: *implantation bleeding*.

It turns out that the moment I was cashing in my check and believing God for His promise was *the very same moment that He was performing it*. And the actual conception? It was the end of February. The same exact month as our ten-year anniversary of trying.

Overwhelmed with all of that information, I sat down for my quiet time, opened my daily *Search the Scriptures* study to the bookmark from the day before, and looked down to that day's reading.

It was parked at Psalm 139. Right where God wanted it.

This is too much, too wonderful—I can't take it all in! I wrote, recording The Message's version of verse six.

He has done His miracle.

He has heard my cry.

He has answered our prayer.

I. Have. Survived. This.

I dug the two positive tests out of the trash and looked again at the still-vibrant pink lines, reminding myself that it wasn't all a dream. That He had perfectly written our story, and we had finally gotten to the best part.

Because I would finally be able to tell the world of our little miracle at *exactly* twelve weeks on Mother's Day, and our babe would be coming into the world right around Thanksgiving—and the anniversary of Shawna's death.

Because He makes all things new.

Because He makes bitter waters sweet.

Because He redeems heartbreak.

Because His mercy is like morning.

Oh, the greatness of His glory.

I RUN MY hand over the page of Psalm 84, remembering. Shawna's spirit is as close in this moment as it was the day we read it together for the first time.

Blessed is the man whose strength is in You, whose heart is set on pilgrimage. As they pass through the Valley of Baca, they make it a spring; the rain also covers it with pools. They go from strength to strength.

The words are familiar. Like the well-loved and threadbare knitted black sweater that used to be my quiet-time robe, I wrap the words warm around me and look back on the valley-turned-wellspring.

Blessed are those whose strength and weight is in and on God. When they pass through the profoundly deep Valley of Baca (Weeping), the paths cut straight through to the profound depths of Him. The Romans 11:33 depths that Paul calls an inexhaustible abundance of riches of both the wisdom of God and the knowledge of Him.

Blessed is the woman whose voice echoes off those Valley-of-Weeping walls, standing in the depths of His depths. *Deep calls out to deep.*

"Ask a sign for yourself from the LORD your God," Isaiah said boldly in chapter 7 of his book. Ask it clear and ask it loud. But pushing further into the Hebrew language reveals that Isaiah's request was something more. Something deeper.

Deepen-ask, he said. Deepen-ask that a miracle may be performed from right there in the valley depths that are found in the depths of Him. Where the deepest part of you is deepen-asking for the deepest part of Him. He could say yes. And He could say no. And He could say nothing at all.

Deep cries out to deep at the noise of Your waterfalls; all Your waves and billows have gone over me. Breaking and rolling and breaking and rolling, taking you deeper so you cry out deeper, rolling every single Valley-of-Weeping burden onto God.

Commit your way to the Lord. When sorrows like sea billows roll, *roll and repose each care of your load on Him.* Transferring the weight off of you and onto Him.

Blessed is she whose strength is in God, and whose weight is billow-rolled right onto Him. Because the storm will blow over and the waves will calm and the heaping sea billows will no longer steamroll you. And you will find yourself rolled up onto the shore—a big, messy heap of relief and survival-joy right there on the sand of His precious thoughts toward you. The ones that are more in number than that sand you're catching your breath on.

Stand up. And look back. Because there will be a heap of stones there, piled up high. Some people like to call them ruins. I like to call them remembrances.

Blessed is she who, passing through the Valley of Baca, makes it a well.

Dig your well. Dig a well that is filled with the fountain spring of God. One that you can return to drink from. One you can bring your children to. A well that the generations after you can come to and pull from, drinking in those depths of the wisdom of God that you dug out. Wisdom from the valley and the waiting and the heartache and the loss. And wisdom from the abundance and provision and joy.

Dig your well.

Notes

CHAPTER 2: WHITE-KNUCKLE FAITH

1. Karen Ehman, "Answer Envy," *Crosswalk.com*, April 29, 2011, https://www.crosswalk.com/devotionals/encouragement/encouragement-for-today-apr-29-2011.html.
2. L.B. Cowman, *Streams in the Desert* (Grand Rapids, MI: Zondervan, 1997), May 24 reading.
3. Cowman, *Streams in the Desert*, May 31 reading.
4. *Matthew Henry's Commentary on the Whole Bible*, "Matthew Henry: Commentary on Job 5," Blue Letter Bible, accessed January 30, 2018, https://www.blueletterbible.org/Comm/mhc/Job/Job_005.cfm?a=441026.

CHAPTER 3: PRONE TO WANDER

1. The phrase "rising up early" is also found in Jeremiah 7:25, 11:7, 25:4, 26:5, 29:19, 32:33, and 35:14-15.
2. Charles H. Spurgeon, "How to Read the Bible" (sermon at the Metropolitan Tabernacle, London, 1879), www.bibleresearcher.com/spurgeon2.html.
3. *Matthew Henry's Commentary on the Whole Bible,* "Matthew Henry: Commentary on Isaiah 59," Blue Letter Bible, accessed February 3, 2018, https://www.blueletterbible.org/Comm/mhc/Isa/Isa_059.cfm?a=738002.
4. Francis Frangipane, *The Three Battlegrounds* (Cedar Rapids, IA: Arrow Publications, 2006), 22.

CHAPTER 4: THE LEARNING GIFT

1. Alan Stibbs, ed., *Search the Scriptures: A Three-Year Daily Devotional Guide to the Whole Bible* (Downers Grove, IL: InterVarsity Press, 2004).

CHAPTER 5: DEEP-VEIN MINING

1. Donald Grey Barnhouse, *God's Glory: Romans 14:13–16:27* (Grand Rapids, MI: Eerdmans, 1964), 18.
2. Beth Moore, *Believing God* (Nashville, TN: B&H Publishing Group, 2015), 21.

CHAPTER 6: DEEP SEA SINGING

1. "Blue Whales and Communication," *National Geographic*, March 26, 2011, http://www.nationalgeographic.com.au/science/blue-whales-and-communication.aspx.

CHAPTER 7: THE RESOURCES

1. Mark Batterson, *Draw the Circle* (Grand Rapids, MI: Zondervan, 2012), Day 30 reading.

SAMPLE STUDY 1: A DAY IN THE LIFE

1. Stibbs, *Search the Scriptures,* 443.

2. A. R. Fausset, "Jamieson, Fausset & Brown: Commentary on 1 Corinthians 12," Blue Letter Bible, accessed February 6, 2018, https://www.blueletterbible.org/Comm/jfb/1Cr/1Cr_012.cfm?a=1074009.

3. *Matthew Henry's Commentary on the Whole Bible,* "Matthew Henry: Commentary on Mark 15," Blue Letter Bible, accessed February 6, 2018, https://www.blueletterbible.org/Comm/mhc/Mar/Mar_015.cfm?a=972043.

4. A.R. Fausset, "Jamieson, Fausset & Brown: Commentary on James 1," Blue Letter Bible, accessed February 6, 2018, https://www.blueletterbible.org/Comm/jfb/Jam/Jam_001.cfm?a=1147005.

5. "Luke 17:5-6," Amplified Bible, footnotes, Biblegateway.com, accessed February 6, 2018, https://www.biblegateway.com/passage/?search=Luke+17%3A5-6+&version=AMP.

6. *Thayer's Greek Lexicon,* Strong's G3735, "oros," https://www.blueletterbible.org/lang/lexicon/lexicon.cfm?Strongs=G3735&t=KJV.

7. *Matthew Henry's Commentary on the Whole Bible,* "Matthew Henry: Commentary on Mark 11," Blue Letter Bible, accessed February 6, 2018, https://www.blueletterbible.org/Comm/mhc/Mar/Mar_011.cfm?a=968023.

SAMPLE STUDY 2: VERSE BY VERSE

1. Charles Spurgeon, *The Treasury of David* (Seattle, WA: Pacific Publishing Studio, 2011), 10.

2. *Gesenius' Hebrew-Chaldee Lexicon,* Strong's H8328, "sheresh," https://www.blueletterbible.org/lang/lexicon/lexicon.cfm?Strongs=H8328&t=KJV.

3. *Matthew Henry's Commentary on the Whole Bible,* "Matthew Henry: Commentary on Psalms 1," Blue Letter Bible, accessed February 6, 2018, https://www.blueletterbible.org/Comm/mhc/Psa/Psa_001.cfm?a=479005.

SAMPLE STUDY 3: REST: A WORD STUDY

1. Mark Batterson, *Draw the Circle* (Grand Rapids, MI: Zondervan, 2012), Day 1 reading.

2. Henry J. van Lennep, *Bible Lands: Their Modern Customs & Manners Illustrative of Scripture* (New York: Harper & Brothers Publishers, 1875), 242.

3. Ann Voskamp, *One Thousand Gifts* (Grand Rapids, MI: Zondervan, 2010), 35.

4. Charles Spurgeon, ed., *The Sword and the Trowel* (London: Passmore & Alabaster, 1873), 81.

EPILOGUE

1. L.B. Cowman, *Streams in the Desert* (Grand Rapids, MI: Zondervan, 1997), March 8 reading.

ACKNOWLEDGMENTS

To say that this book was a labor of love is, quite possibly, the most extreme kind of an understatement. It has taken a village to see this book-babe through her gestation, and its very existence comes with the most grateful and humble thanks to:

Shawna, your friendship always was and will forever be absolutely irreplaceable to me. Thank you for leading me to your well and then teaching me to dig my own.

Josh, your unwavering faith is what kept me grounded those ten years. And your unending love and support throughout this process kept me going when I wanted to quit. Thank you for loving me the way you do. Our love story is my most favorite.

The Banasek and Johnson families, for believing in us as we chose to do the crazy thing.

Emily M., Emily W., Jaimee, Jill, Krista, Kristen, and Selena, for holding my weary arms up daily and battling on your knees in prayer on my behalf.

Mandy, for sticking your neck out for me. Kara, for getting up before dawn with me.

Kristen, Tiffany, and Mindy, for being obedient to share your dreams and visions and breathing life into my waiting-sails.

Hannah and Karen, for showing me the ropes and never tiring of my questions.

Don, for always having my back.

Shelby, for sharing our crazy story. Kathleen, for reaching out and cheering me on. Janelle, for bringing my (very) particular design vision for this book to life. And to the entire Harvest House team for investing in me.

And to the Lord—my God, and my King—for meeting me faithfully at our morning perch. For continually whispering hope. For anchoring me tightly into the depths of You. And for never letting go. I love how You love me. And I will never tire of the way Your Spirit speaks to me.

ABOUT THE AUTHOR

JANE JOHNSON is a writer, designer, photographer, speaker, and Scripture-digger who is caught in a passionate love affair with the Word of God. She lives on a tropical island in the middle of the Pacific with her overly handsome husband and perfect miracle babe.

Thousands do life with her on her website, where you can find more Bible studies, devotionals, photographic chroniclings, and almost-daily writings: janejohnson.com.